YOUR
VOICE

In our *Paperfront* series

Sample Social Speeches
Wedding Speeches
The Public Speaker's Joke Book

YOUR VOICE

How to enrich it
and develop it for
speaking, acting and
everyday conversation

ANDREW ARMITAGE

RIGHT WAY

Typeset in 11½pt Times Roman by One and a Half Graphics, Redhill, Surrey. Printed and bound in Great Britain by Cox & Wyman Ltd., Reading, Berkshire.

The *Right Way* series and the *Paperfronts* series are both published by Elliot Right Way Books, Brighton Road, Lower Kingswood, Tadworth, Surrey, KT20 6TD, U.K.

CONTENTS

To Mickey and Bean,

who lived with it.

INTRODUCTION

If words are the clothes of thought, then the voice is their wardrobe mistress. And the wardrobe mistress who's skilled in her art will make her charges look just as she wishes them to look. A subtle change here and a dash of colour there might alter the whole impression that a character makes on the audience. The addition or subtraction of a garment can speak much.

So, too, with the voice.

The voice, as we shall see, works in concert with other parts of the body to create a complex ensemble of communication. But even when it stands alone — as does the voice of radio — it can do far more than speak words.

Words, after all, can be spoken by a voice synthesiser. But you'd feel cheated if such a device were used instead of actors in a radio play. They, after all, do far more than merely utter those phonic shapes we call the spoken word.

In this book on getting the best out of your voice, I've tried to work on two levels: making you aware of the parts of you that work together to create that piece of magic we call the voice; and suggesting exercises to help you to tone up those parts and keep them in good working order.

And you can begin right now. You may have noticed already that the style I've chosen to write in is very speakable. I'm using contractions (for instance 'I'm' for 'I am' and 'we'd' for 'we had' and 'we would'), just as we do in everyday speech. It's not slovenly to do this; merely a way of making speech more articulate.

I'm also using sentences that aren't made cumbersome with subordinate clauses. This is not to suggest that you're incapable of making sense of such sentences. After all, we read complex sentences every day in books and some newspapers. But when we speak we use sentence structures that are quite different from the written word.

So I'm asking you to try to read this book at times when you won't feel too self-conscious about reading aloud. As you do read, try to hear your voice, its rises and falls, its changes in volume and pace, its pauses. From this moment, be aware of your voice both when reading aloud and in conversation, whether it's formal conversation in a meeting or a chat with friends over dinner or a drink.

When you come to the exercises, you'll *have* to read aloud, of course, but you can accustom yourself to the pleasurable activity of doing so right now. As you read, imagine that you're not only making sense of the words for yourself but for another, for an imaginary listener (or a real one if someone's willing to listen).

I'll ask you to use text often throughout the book, some of it easy to read and some more difficult.

Chapter One will familiarise you with some of the workings of what are called the 'organs of articulation' — those bits and pieces I mentioned a moment ago that work to produce vocal sounds and shapes. Then we'll work on specifics: the vowels and consonants, effective breathing and relaxation and ironing out some common speech problems.

There's a chapter devoted entirely to exercise, and you'll find there examples of the English language as spoken now and several hundred years ago. The reason for this will be explained.

We end with a chapter devoted to the art of public speaking. This has been deliberately left until last because the book is primarily about giving your voice a workout and discovering new possibilities. But many of us look at voice improvement with a view to using our voices in public, and if you are one of those people then Chapter Nine will give you a handy introduction to the subject of public speaking and, I hope, will whet your appetite for some of the many books devoted to the subject.

Finally, a point about sexism — or what I hope will be the lack of it. Many writers argue that, rather than encumber their prose with such phrases as 'him or her' or 'he or she', they'll just use the masculine and make it do for both. In this book — on the rare occasion when the personal pronoun is needed — I've chosen one sex or the other, and hope they'll have balanced out by the end.

1.
IN A MANNER OF SPEAKING
Your voice and how you use it

You've arrived home from work. You're a little tired, but looking forward to an evening out with friends. You shower and put on fresh clothes. If you're a man you probably have a shave. Already you're feeling much better. You go to the bedroom and put on a little makeup or splash on some aftershave, you comb your hair. As you prepare to leave the house you glance at yourself in the hall mirror, to make sure your appearance is just so.

You've done all of this without thinking about it. Your mind's on the evening ahead, after all. Anyway, what is there to think about? Haven't you gone through the same procedure a thousand and one times before? Of course you have.

But hang on a minute. Before you step into the street, go back into the lounge for a few moments and go through some vowel and consonant exercises. Then lie on the floor and go through a relaxation session, before getting up and giving your breathing a workout.

The idea seems absurd to us, and yet we've just gone to the trouble of making ourselves look, smell and feel good. What's wrong with *sounding* good, too? Why should the voice be left out? After all, it's our primary mode of communication.

You wouldn't, of course, do voice exercises at that inconvenient time of the day, but I think the above scenario makes the point.

We just don't think about our voices.

AN EXTRA DIMENSION OF MEANING

I became fascinated with the spoken word during the 1970s when I was taking a speech and drama course. I became exhilarated by the thought that a word can be invested with so much more than its dictionary definition. I began to notice how something as seemingly insignificant as a pause or a change of pace would add a new dimension of meaning to a simple statement.

Try a little experiment for yourself right now. Say the following sentence quickly and with the same interval between the words.

This moment is very beautiful.

Now say it again, but pause for just a second before the word 'is'. By the addition of a short pause, you've allowed the power of the word 'moment' to gather before being released. With no pause, the word was lost. It was merely one of five words making up a simple statement.

It's a bit like waiting for the charge to accumulate in your camera's flash unit before discharging it in a blinding blaze of light. If you don't wait long enough, the flash may be more like a damp squib.

Not all words need this sort of treatment. If you were reading out the instructions on how to fill in your income tax return or wire up a plug you would probably find very little to excite you. But imagine reading a piece of good prose or verse in the same instructional tones, and you would agree with me that it would be dull stuff indeed.

Pausing before or after a word to give it emphasis is

called 'pointing' a word, giving it force. An increase in volume is another way of pointing, and so is a sudden rise in pitch or a gesture of the hand or arm. But pointing isn't the only way to make speech more attractive. You'll also find such expressiveness in the *music* of the voice, its rise and fall. And of course you need to be clear. The vowels and consonants must be right.

To get the best out of your voice you need to feel relaxed. Tension gathers mostly in the upper part of the body, around the neck, throat and shoulders. This restricts a good flow of air. Then there's the question of posture. I don't mean walking about with a cushion on your head to practise deportment, but merely feeling that your posture is comfortable and isn't causing any constrictions in the air passages.

If you ever find yourself speaking in a noisy environment or from a rostrum to a group or gathering, you'll need to consider projection. Projection isn't just shouting. Listen to an actor speak from a stage. He makes his voice heard at the back of the auditorium, even when he's whispering sweet things into the ear of his stage lover or mumbling to himself in a soliloquy. He uses one of several techniques for projecting the voice and making it carry without actually bellowing. We'll discuss these later.

THE ORGANS OF ARTICULATION

This is just a fancy way of referring to the bits and pieces of our anatomy that contribute to the quality of our spoken words. But a word of warning here: never lose sight of the fact that you don't so much *have* a voice as *are* a voice. You're a walking system of communication. Your voice reflects much about you — your environment, your background, your physical size, your temperament, your mood of the moment. We can take the old saying, 'It's not *what* you say: it's the way you say it' a stage further by adding, '... and your ability to *control* the way you say it.'

Think how often you've detected that a friend is in a particular mood. You may not have seen her — just heard her voice behind you or over the telephone. You detect that she's a little off, perhaps, and don't really know how you knew. But the chances are that it's something in the voice. By becoming more aware of how the voice works, you can go some way to controlling the effect your voice is having on others.

But let's move on and have a look at just what produces the physical voice. Although the voice is a product of both body and mind, it's the bodily bits we'll be looking at in some detail in the following chapters.

Let's begin with the lungs. We take in air, the motive force behind speech. The lungs aren't balloons, but a greyish, spongy, elastic tissue filled with many tiny chambers. They expel their air through the trachea, or windpipe. But the lungs are not themselves muscles. They're acted upon by the diaphragm and the intercostal muscles between the ribs.

When the air is expelled, it begins its journey through the trachea and passes to the larynx, which contains the vocal cords, which are sometimes referred to as vocal folds. The area between them is called the glottis. When the cords are brought together they form a partial obstacle to the air, which has to push itself through, causing them to vibrate. But that vibration isn't enough in itself to generate an appreciable sound.

Consider for a moment the tuning fork. You twang the prongs and they vibrate, but you can barely hear that vibration until you touch a surface, such as a desktop, with the handle. Consider also the guitar and violin. You strike the strings with plectrum or bow, but it's the box that amplifies the vibrations and makes them audible and gives them tone and colour. The desktop and the box are the resonators.

The upper end of the body has a number of resonating cavities that catch that vibration and amplify it. The mouth itself is one, of course. The sinuses play a part, and so does the pharynx, which sits above the larynx. The pharynx is the first resonating cavity. The chest, too, is a resonator, as you can hear if you stand close to a particularly deeply-spoken man and notice that some of the lower resonance is actually coming from there.

Each resonator makes its own contribution to the end result and, because we're all built differently, the resonators play a large part in determining our individual vocal characteristics, giving us our own particular 'sound'.

But let's continue our journey. The air is now in the mouth, and it's vibrating. It's at a particular pitch, determined by how tight or loose the vocal cords were when it struck them. But it's still only sound. It's about to be made into a recognisable shape by the movement of various parts of the mouth: the tongue, the soft palate and the lips. Other parts of the mouth play a rôle, too, but they're rigid. These are the hard palate, the teeth and the alveolar ridge.

The hard palate is the roof of the mouth and the alveolar ridge (or 'tooth ridge', as it's sometimes called) is the hard ridge just behind the top front teeth. The soft palate is behind the hard palate, and meets the back of the tongue to trap air for the sound of k. Its anatomical name is 'velum'.

(Don't worry too much about technical terms at this stage. Those who want to learn them will find the glossary useful at the end of the book.)

It's by the various movements of parts of the mouth that we form vowels, and the *positions* of those parts of the mouth in relation to others that give us our consonants. We'll look in more detail at what does what in the next chapter.

So far we've taken a brief look at the making of words —

a most eloquent form of communication we take so much for granted because our native tongue comes so easily and naturally to us.

THE ORIGINS OF SPEECH

Language is an evolved phenomenon, of course, and even today researchers will argue over precisely how it came about. Even within each individual, language forms over a period of years. But looked at in its most basic sense it's a method of influencing our environment by making noises.

When you were a baby you soon realised that certain noises elicited specific responses from your parents. This phenomenon probably began with crying to be fed. You began to associate these noises with getting what you wanted, and so formed the habit of making them. But soon the learning process changed, and your mode of expression gradually became more structured. Words began to form. Then the words would become the components of recognisable sentence structures.

And so the process continued — and continues at a less accelerated rate even today, as you add to your vocabulary through reading and listening.

It's easy to see why we take speech for granted. Something that's acquired more quickly, such as a new skill associated with your work, would not be treated so casually. You would nurture it, improve and polish it through conscious practice.

And our *laissez-faire* attitude to our vocal makeup has left us with the need to bring conscious practice to bear on our voices, too, if we are able to make improvements and inject more life and expressiveness into our speech.

Before going on to the exercises in subsequent chapters, I want you to read aloud the piece of prose I've reproduced below. Read it into a taperecorder if possible. If you don't have one, then ask a caring friend or relative to listen critically. Ask her to make notes, because when you've finished reading the book and doing the exercises she's going to have to listen again, because you'll be asked to come back to the same passage and read it with the benefit of greater awareness of your vocal capabilities. If it's a taperecorder and not a friend that you're using, record the second attempt *after* the first attempt (in other words, don't wipe the first one), and make a comparison.

If you're fortunate enough to have both a taperecorder and a willing friend, then so much the better.

Get your friend or equipment ready, adopt a reasonably relaxed and easy posture, either standing or sitting on a hardbacked chair, and read ...

So many people pass this way so many times. I often wonder what occupies their minds as they walk, some slowly with the gait of old men, some briskly with a destination to reach. The grass under their feet is soft and lush at this time of year. It's a good time, the early autumn, even on dull days like today. The colours are so much more interesting in the autumn than in the summer. 'Season of mists and mellow fruitfulness' indeed! Or, as Shakespeare would have it, 'the teeming autumn, big with rich increase.' I fancy that as much has been written of autumn as of any of the other seasons. But what's that? Engines? Who could dream of invading the quiet of a day such as this? Here they come. *Motorbikes!* One, two, three ... *six* of them, over the brow of that grassy hill. Leather-clad men with shiny helmets, revving the angry engines impatiently, scattering the walkers, some of whom are raising their fists in anger. Round and round they go, the bikes, churning up the grass, throwing soil into the air. And they're leaving. The way they

came. Over that hill. Into the distance goes their growling, till it becomes a mere whine. Some of the walkers are tut-tutting, but happy that the interruption is over. They continue their perambulations as though nothing had invaded their tranquil day.

You'll be aware of a change of direction, as it were, in the middle — a change of pace that should change your delivery. But that's as much as I'm going to help you for now, because, when you come back to it, it'll be with a different idea, we hope, of your vocal skills.

2.

MIND YOUR Ps AND Qs
Consonants –
the mortar between the bricks

Consonants, as we know, are all the letters that aren't vowels. They determine the beginnings and ends of words, and in some cases enable vowel sounds to change direction in the middle of words.

Perhaps I'm stating the obvious, but it's surprising how many people speak indistinctly because they don't pay enough attention to crisp consonants. Try saying the word 'kaput' without the consonants, and you'd be left with something like 'ah-uh'.

So in this chapter we'll look at all the consonants and some combinations of consonants, and make ourselves aware of what's happening to the organs of articulation.

Awareness of what's happening in there is half the battle. If you have a particular weakness with, say, your **f** and **v** sounds, you can begin to correct it by knowing what's *supposed* to be happening, and making sure it *does* happen. Your consonants may be clear in every way, and you could skip this chapter and move to the one on vowels. But I hope you'll stick with it because we're making an exploration of the mouth.

Although I've split the consonants from the vowels and

put them into two separate chapters for analytical convenience, the two really do belong to each other in a mutually beneficial way, and we need both in order to concentrate on either one; and in our exercises you'll no doubt find some overlapping disciplines.

LACKING CONFIDENCE IN SPEECH

Why do some people speak indistinctly? Why do they find difficulty in articulating, making their consonants clear and crisp? We often talk loosely of a 'laziness' in speech, but it's rarely the kind of laziness we refer to when we talk of not wanting to get off our backsides to feed the cat or wash the dishes. That kind of laziness would make us not want to speak in the first place.

Indistinct consonants are often associated with a lack of confidence. We are perhaps unsure of ourselves, so our thoughts are not being carried through effectively into speech. It's as though we wanted to talk but were afraid of what we are saying, so we speak through a veil or curtain, hoping in a strange sort of way that what we say isn't really being heard lest our inadequacies of thought should be found out.

This lack of confidence in what we have to say may have been with us since we first learned to speak. After all, our peculiarities of speech, the things that make us all sound different, are largely bound up with environment. That environment begins in infancy, as we discussed in the first chapter. We come to know which noises elicit certain reactions.

Some people *hear* sound more distinctly than others, and so the sound they make by imitation is going to depend on their perception of the sound they're imitating. If you don't hear speech too clearly, perhaps you won't reproduce it too clearly. And not hearing speech may not necessarily be an inadequacy of your hearing, but of your concentration on what's being said and how by the person you're listening to, be it a newsreader or a friend.

Uncrisp consonants, then, are often the fault of lack of confidence, or not being aware that our consonants *should* be crisper than they are. Rarely is it an inability to use the parts of the mouth that co-operate with each other in the production of those consonants. There may be a weakness there, but not an inability. And weaknesses can be eliminated with exercise.

Some people actually overdo their consonants, of course, making their point with moist emphasis that has their listeners discreetly wiping their faces with the backs of fingers. This, too, would be a speech fault. You need to find the happy medium.

It's weak consonants, though, that are the most common fault, and I'm going to ask you to perform the other fault, overemphasis, in order to beef them up a little.

We're back to that question of awareness. At first, exaggerate, then bring the energy down to an acceptable level. You'll probably find, if you listen back to yourself from tape, that your consonants weren't that exaggerated, anyway, because they were perhaps a little weak to begin with.

THE ANATOMY OF A CONSONANT

Whatever the reason for this indistinctness, it can be remedied — unless, of course, there's something physically wrong with part of the mouth. We can form new habits and ditch old ones. First, though, we need to know what makes a consonant happen.

There are three stages to the making of a consonant:

1. Two organs of articulation (such as top and bottom lip or teeth and tongue) come together;

2. Air is released by the lungs and comes through the mouth;
3. It moves through or around those organs to produce a sound peculiar to their positioning.

In the case of a plosive consonant, such as a **t** or a **b**, air is held for a moment before release. In the case of a continuant, such as **l** or **n**, air merely has to find a way out. With **n** it comes through the nose because the mouth is closed off. With **l** it comes from the sides of the tongue, which are held down while the tip is up. **L** is often referred to as a lateral consonant, because the air's coming out sideways.

Now, if the muscularity of the articular organs is weak, or the coming together is mistimed, you get an indistinct consonant. As we go through the consonants, make a mental note of how the sound is being produced. First, though, a word about the different types of consonant.

Consonants come in two categories: voiced and unvoiced. **V**, for instance, is the voiced version of **f**. **T** is the *un*voiced version of **d**. **K** and **g** (a hard **g**, as in 'goal') are also formed by the same parts of the mouth, but the first is unvoiced and the second is voiced. **Sh** is the unvoiced version of the soft **g**, as in 'genre', and **ch** is the unvoiced version of **dj**, as it occurs at both ends of 'judge'.

Into each of these two categories come two subcategories: consonants, as we saw just a while ago, are plosive or continuant. A plosive consonant, as its name suggests, forms a small explosion. **P**, for instance, is made by holding air behind the lips, preventing it from breaking out of the mouth, and then letting it out with a small explosion. Both **p** and **b** are plosives, as are **t, d, k** and the hard **g**.

Continuants are so called because they're not restricted in the same way: they're able to continue. The **m**, for instance, can be held for as long as the breath allows. So can the **n** and the **l**.

Other consonants come somewhere between the two. You could make a case for being able to hold a **w** for a long time, but the consonant isn't really fully formed until the lips have opened and the following vowel has begun. Until that happens, **w** is just **oo**.

Let's begin with the consonants that are formed at the front of the mouth, and work our way backwards. Pronounce the different consonants aloud as we come to them, adding 'ah' to give you 'pah', 'bah', 'kah' and so on. Say them slowly and deliberately, having first opened the mouth slightly so you can feel it move into position for the consonant you're speaking. Then leave a few seconds with the mouth open, and move it into position for the next one.

Stand in front of a mirror, and watch your mouth carefully. You won't be able to see all that happens, but the sounds that require an open mouth will allow you to see the movements of the tongue, teeth and lips.

P and **B**   These are formed by the lips holding back air that's straining to get out. When you let it out, there's a small explosion of sound. The first is unvoiced, and releases just air; the second is voiced and releases air and vocal sound.

M   This is formed by the same lip positions, but air is diverted down the nose while the lips are held together. **M** takes slightly longer to say than **p** or **b**.

W   This is about as close as a consonant comes to being a vowel, and, indeed, at the end of a word such as 'window' it merely directs us to combine it with the **o** to say 'oh'. But it's stronger at the beginning and middle of words, and is formed by pushing the lips forward as if for 'oo', and then opening to let the sound out unimpeded.

T and **D**   This pair are formed when the tongue is placed at the back of what's known as the alveolar ridge, and air is trapped and suddenly released.

L   The tip of the tongue is again touching the alveolar ridge, but the sides of the tongue are dropped, allowing air to come through. First say **t** and then **l**, and feel the difference in tongue position at the sides. (Let's make a distinction here between the two types of l — light and dark. A light l usually comes at the beginning and middle of a word, when just the tip of the tongue is in contact with the upper part of the mouth: the ridge. The dark l is more likely at the end of a word or just after a consonant, as in 'bottle'. The main difference is that the *back* of the tongue is slightly higher, and it's this closeness of it to the soft palate that gives us our difference in sound. Try the two sounds for yourself and try to etch onto your memory just what the difference is.)

N   Here, the tongue adopts the same position as for **l**, but we allow the air to come down the nose by bringing the teeth into contact with the sides of the tongue, thereby blocking off the air.

M   Although both **m** and **n** are nasal consonants, the **n** relies on having the tongue tip touching the top of the mouth, and the lips open, whereas the **m** has the lips closed and the tongue at rest, allowing vibration in both nose and mouth. By lowering the tongue, you've effectively enlarged the cavity of the mouth, and this has made the sound 'bigger', and distinguishable from **n**.

TH   This is another one made at the front of the mouth, but this time by placing the tip of the tongue between both sets of teeth lightly enough to allow air to escape, but tightly enough to impede the flow. The resultant friction gives us the unvoiced **th**, as in 'thin'. The same positions occur in the voiced version, which gives us 'those' and 'this'.

F and **V**   These are fricative consonants, too. The same principles apply here, but the sound's made by the top teeth and bottom lip. One is unvoiced, the other voiced.

S and **Z**   These are made in a similar way to **t**, but air is allowed to move down the centre of the tongue, escaping through a small gap at the front and creating a hiss or, in the case of **Z**, a buzz.

R   Form **s**, and then curl the tip of the tongue back, and you have **r**.

CH   This occurs at the beginning of 'chop' and really is a combination of two consonants: **t** and **sh**.

DJ   This is the voiced version of **ch**.

G   We usually speak of the hard **g**, as it occurs
              in 'go', and the soft **g** of 'George'. But there's
              another — the 'supersoft' **g** in 'genre'. The
              supersoft **g** is the voiced version of **sh**.
              When we pronounce the slightly harder **dj**,
              we find that the tongue, as for **tch**, touches
              the ridge and adds a hardness to the sound.

Y   This is another consonant used as a vowel —
              and, indeed, in some languages, such as
              Welsh, it *is* a vowel. When it's a consonant,
              however, the middle of the tongue
              approximates to the top of your mouth, but
              the tip is tucked behind the bottom front
              teeth. What starts as a channel at the back
              of the tongue opens out as the tongue begins
              to turn downwards.

K and **G** We saw **g** in its softer forms above. To form
              the hard **g**, the back of the tongue and the
              soft palate come together for a plosive. The
              same happens with **k**, but unvoiced.

NG   It's often missed off the ends of the words
              giving us monstrosities such as 'comin'' and
              'goin''. This, too, is formed at the back of
              the mouth, with the same positions as for
              the hard **g**. But air is allowed to come down
              the nose, to form a nasal consonant, like **n**.
              In fact, looked at like that it really is like an
              n, but formed with the back of the tongue
              rather than the front.

Ch   Not to be confused with **CH** above. This is the guttural. We don't find the guttural used in English words, but that doesn't mean we never need to pronounce it. Often we might refer to a Scottish loch or the composer Bach. Or we may be called upon to mention the Welsh town of Harlech. This is formed in the same way as **k**, but in the way of a fricative — in other words, allowing air to escape with friction by opening up a small gap between the back of the tongue and the soft palate.

CRISP CONSONANTS MEAN POSITIVE SPEECH

Used in a very exaggerated way, consonants can be made to sound threatening: 'Look! I don't want to know — okay?' Say that with soft consonants, then with hard. While we don't need to use them in quite that way in most of our social intercourse, we must at least *be able to* if called upon in a speaking situation to be emphatic.

Anyway, exaggeration is what we're about in these exercises, in order to enable you to hone your awareness of your organs of articulation.

Go through the consonants above again, exaggerating the muscular activity needed to produce them. Then speak each one soft and hard alternately.

As well as the weak **ng** we encountered above, there's another consonant that's often left out. It's **t** — especially at the end of a word. So, 'Put it out' becomes 'Pu' i' ou'.' And there'll be a glottal stop instead of a **t**. A glottal stop — which we discuss in more detail in Chapter Four — is a trapping of air in the glottis, or opening between the vocal cords. When we bring the vocal cords together in our larynx, but stop short of uttering a sound, we create a glottal stop. Go one further, and release the sound, and we have a plosive consonant that just doesn't occur in the English tongue — except through laziness.

Try it now, just to get the feel of it. Begin to breathe out, but trap the air in the throat.

You can hear the glottal stop used by speakers of the Yorkshire dialect, who often miss out the word 'the'. But listen carefully: they're not merely missing it out, but adding something almost indefinable — a little trapping of air in the throat where 'the' would be. Let's represent that trapping of air — or glottal stop — by an exclamation mark for a moment. Thus, 'I'm just off to the pub' becomes 'I'm just off to !pub'. What they're really doing is substituting it for the letter **t**, because, as we know, Yorkshire dialect reduces the word 'the' to a mere **t**; the **t** then becomes a glottal stop.

Within the context of the Yorkshire dialect, this is perfectly all right, and, as a Yorkshireman myself, I wouldn't dream of criticising the practice. But that is a matter of dialect, and what we're discussing here is speech *faults*.

So let's return to the phrase above, 'put it out'. Usually, provided we're not in a huge echoey room or trying to speak above a loud noise, we can be understood if we substitute a glottal stop for **t**, but it's far from satisfactory. It sounds awful and is no substitute for using the consonant **t**.

Now we'll do some more exercises. They're designed to do two things:

1. To make you more aware through repetition of which bits are doing what inside your mouth and throat; and

2. To get you into the habit of forming crisp consonants by constant repetition and the strengthening and toning up of the muscles that drive the organs of articulation.

Say the following syllables rhythmically, using three groups of four followed by a long one at the end. You can invent your own rhythms eventually, but this will do to be going on with. And remember to exaggerate, so you really *feel* the pressure of one part of the mouth against the other, the vibrations in the mouth and nose and the small explosions on the plosives.

PA PA PA PA	PA PA PA PA	PA PA PA PA	PAH
BA BA BA BA	BA BA BA BA	BA BA BA BA	BAH
WA WA WA WA	WA WA WA WA	WA WA WA WA	WAH
MA MA MA MA	MA MA MA MA	MA MA MA MA	MAH
NA NA NA NA	NA NA NA NA	NA NA NA NA	NAH
TA TA TA TA	TA TA TA TA	TA TA TA TA	TAH
DA DA DA DA	DA DA DA DA	DA DA DA DA	DAH

You'll notice that, once again, we've begun at the front of the mouth and then progressed to the back. Do the same now with the other consonants in the order they were introduced in the list starting on page 23. Then go the other way, starting with the back-of-the-mouth consonants and moving to the front. Keep to the front of your mind an awareness of what's happening, and carry that awareness through to everyday speech.

You may have found you couldn't say this exercise very fast at first, especially on the **ng** and guttural **ch**. But, as you continue, you'll find that you're able to speed up and still make each consonant distinct from its neighbour. If it *isn't* distinct, slow down until you get it right, and then increase the speed at which you do the exercise.

SLURRING

Another reason for indistinct consonants is the slurring

of one into another. The phrase 'in another', for instance, is quite difficult to say, because there's a tendency to slur. Try saying 'imagine an animal' very quickly. Did you slur? Did the middle word disappear from the sentence? If so, slow right down, and gradually speed up until each **n** is distinct.

Now I'm going to make things a little more difficult for you by putting the consonant at the end of the **AH** rather than at the beginning. So, using the order above, let's go through them again ...

AP AP AP AP	AP AP AP AP	AP AP AP AP	AHP
AB AB AB AB	AB AB AB AB	AB AB AB AB	AHB
AW AW AW AW	AW AW AW AW	AW AW AW AW	AHW
(as in 'cow')			

... and so on. What you must do is resist the temptation to carry the consonant from one of these 'words' into the next. Do it once, though, and see what happens. If someone walked into the room while you were in the middle of the line, they wouldn't know whether you were saying 'ab' or 'ba' until you reached the end of the line and ended on either a vowel or a consonant.

So try them again, stopping at the end of each 'word' for a moment before moving on to the next. You won't be able to do this very quickly at first but, again, begin slowly and gradually speed up.

You've now begun to introduce some agility into the muscles of the mouth. Just as a workout in a gym is about more than just building brute strength, so is a workout for the voice. The gym exercises will, or should, also make you supple and agile. The idea of voice exercises is that they'll do just that for the mouth and its various bits of vocal equipment.

When you've gone through the exercises above several

times, taking them right through the list of consonants from the front of the mouth to the back and then the other way, try this next one. It's a little more difficult. We're going to put the consonants at the front *and* back of the vowel sounds ...

PAP PAP PAP PAP   PAP PAP PAP PAP   PAP PAP PAP PAP   PAHP

BAB BAB BAB BAB   BAB BAB BAB BAB   BAB BAB BAB BAB   BAHB

... and so on, through 'MAM', 'SAS', 'LAL', 'SHASH', 'JAJ' (both as in 'judge' and as in 'genre') and all the rest until you come to the guttural 'CHACH'. Feel the **p**s popping off the lips, the crispness of the **k**, the liquid **l** and the sibilant **s**. Feel the vibration in the mouth as you say **m** and in the nose with **n**. Feel the friction of **f** and the vibrating **v** on the bottom lip.

We'll end with some exercises. If there are some specific problems with your consonants, such as an **s** that's too sibilant or an **r** that's formed at the back of the tongue (the so-called uvular **r**), then you'll find special exercises in Chapter Four.

EXERCISES FOR THE ORGANS OF ARTICULATION

The lips
Say the following, exaggerating the **p**, **b**, **m** and **w** sounds.

Please pass the pencils and pens, Papa.

Peter Piper picked a peck of pickled pepper. If Peter Piper picked a peck of pickled pepper, where's the peck of pickled pepper Peter Piper picked?

Betty Botter bought some butter but she said, 'This butter's bitter!'

Bow to the boy who brought the bales.

While Willy walked with Walter we watched the whales waging war.

Imagine an imaginary menagerie manager imagining managing an imaginary menagerie.

Minnie and Mary Minnow munched more mouthfuls.

The tongue
Now try the following ...

Theophilus Thistle the thistle-sifter had a sieve of unsifted thistles and a sieve of sifted thistles, but Theophilus Thistle the thistle-sifter thoughtlessly thrust a thistle through the thick of his thumb.

Tell Terry Tucker and Tommy Tattler not to tell tales.

Nanny nudged Nicola.

Ten tons didn't arrive.

Rory Roberts raced rats around the ring.

Did Danny Deever die?

Lanky Lily Lallingham lolled languidly.

So swanky Sarah saw the sailing ships — so what?

Back of the tongue and soft palate

Kick cake and coke quite quickly.

Go to the gig and gag the gargling gargoyle.

Get gum quickly and go great guns in August.

With his crooked finger the king was cracking the pink Ming.

King Canute could not control the coming tide.

Gloria gladly crashed the gong and struck the glockenspiel.

Now some general exercises for vocal agility. You'll notice that some of them make you jump from one part of the mouth to another in quick succession.

Come, McCluskie, make many men man the mainsail.

Tippety tat tat, tippety tap.

Pippety pat, pippety pat, tippety tap, tippety tap, pippety tap.

Fee fie fo fum.

Fry fake food for Freddie Ferguson.

Five very fine valiant footmen.

KA-KA NA-NA MA-MA	MA-MA NA-NA KA-KA
NA-NA KA-KA MA MA	TA-TA-DA-DA-SA-SA
MA-MA-NA-NA-LA-LA	FA-FA-VA-VA-FA-FA
FA-VA-FA-VA	VA-FA-VA-FA
TA-DA-DA-TA-TA-DA-DA	TAMMA MATTA MATTA TAMMA

RALLA LARRA RALLA LARRA

It takes little imagination to invent your own, once you're aware of the principles involved and what it is you're trying to make your mouth do. As with all the exercises in this book, begin slowly and gently, and gradually increase in pace until you feel confident that you've made some improvement.

Not everyone will find all the exercises difficult, of course. Some mouths are more agile in certain areas than others. Once you've established where your weaknesses are, try to concentrate on the exercises that address those weaknesses. But do make sure you *know* your weaknesses. Often, we don't hear ourselves as others hear us. So try a taperecorder or a patient friend. Preferably both.

After any exercise session, pick up a piece of text and read it aloud. Exaggerate at first, then bring the energy level down to normal. Remember: you're working on sharpening awareness as well as toning up the muscles and creating new — and good — habits of speech.

We've looked at the mortar between the building blocks. It's time now to turn our attention to the building blocks themselves.

3.

SHAPING UP
The value of vowels

If consonants are the mortar, then the vowels are the bricks
or the building blocks of speech. In the last chapter we
filleted the word 'kaput' by taking out its consonants, and
were left with 'ah-uh'. Take away its vowels and you could
be left with 'cop it' or even 'keep out'.

But before we go any further, let me make it clear that,
although we're discussing vowels in this chapter — the very
shapes of our words — I'm not going to be recommending
that you change your natural accent.

In days gone by it was thought unrefined to speak with
any accent other than standard southern English. We
sometimes call this 'received pronunciation' or 'RP'. You
hear RP spoken by BBC newsreaders, but gone are the days
when all broadcasters spoke like that. These days, you hear
a rich mixture of accents, not only from all parts of the UK,
but from other English-speaking countries.

Some actors, even, will prefer to hang on to their native
regional accent, no doubt believing that to change what is
naturally theirs is to lose some of the vitality of their
speech, and to sound a little 'off' will give it a degree of
virility. But the thing to remember is that it's not wrong to
wish to keep your accent, and nor is it wrong to wish to

change it. In some circles, an accent approximating to RP puts you at a distinct advantage when such things as promotion or being offered a job are on the agenda.

Some people's accents change when they move to another part of the country, while others' remain stubbornly the same. So we're not talking here about the 'how-now-brown-cow' school of elocution, but shaping our vowels in a way that allows us to be understood by the fellow from Inverness, the lad from Aberystwyth or the woman from East Kent. A particularly harsh or thick accent needs moderating, but that won't necessarily rob it of its richness.

A few words from Dr Johnson will sum up our observations on accent:

> **A small intermixture of provincial peculiarities may, perhaps, have an agreeable effect, as the notes of different birds concur in the harmony of the grove, and please more than if they were all exactly alike.**

When we speak of vowels in this book, we'll also be including vowel *sounds* in our consideration. After all, we're told that there are but five vowels in English, **a**, **e**, **i**, **o** and **u**. But what is a **y** at the end of 'very' but a vowel? Similarly, the **w** at the end of a word contributes to its vowel sound, as in 'drew' or 'window'.

Exercises for vowels aren't as obvious as those for consonants. With consonants you can feel what's happening in your mouth far more easily, because flesh and teeth are coming together in various combinations. The vowels work differently. Your mouth adopts just one shape for a simple vowel, and for a more complex vowel sound it adopts a shape and changes that shape during the course of the syllable. It's for this reason that when we come to the vowel exercises it'll be important to exaggerate to get the feel of and remember what's happening in the mouth.

Vowel sounds are split conveniently for us into three distinct types: pure (involving no movement of the mouth once it's been engaged for that particular sound), diphthongs (one movement) and triphthongs (two movements). Looked at another way, pure vowels have one shape, diphthongs have two and triphthongs have three.

THE VOWEL SCALE

Pure vowels are:

1.	**EE**	peace
2.	**i**	pick
3.	**e**	bed
4.	**a**	mass
5.	**AH**	rather
6.	**o**	rock
7.	**AW**	lawn
8.	**oo**	book
9.	**OO**	fool
10.	**NEUTRAL**	po(e)m, lin(e)n or (a)bout
11.	**u**	bun
12.	**ER**	firm

Diphthongs are:

13.	**OH**	note
14.	**AY**	fame
15.	**I**	ice
16.	**OW**	doubt
17.	**OI**	employ
18.	**EW**	suit
19.	**AIR**	wear
20.	**OOR**	sure
21.	**EAR**	weird

And triphthongs are:

22.	**URE**	mural
23.	**OUR**	sour
24.	**IRE**	shire

(Notice that I've employed lowercase letters for shorter sounds, to avoid confusion between the **i** in 'bid' and the **I** in 'size' for instance, or the **a** in 'fat' and the **AH** in 'father'.)

The above lists cover just about every possible vowel sound. There are arguments centring on whether the word 'power' should have the same vowel shape as 'sour', but it's so easy to become pedantic about such things. If you wish to see 'tower' as two distinct syllables (which, strictly speaking, it is) then that's fine. Most elocution teachers would lump the two.

Let's now look at what the mouth is doing to form some of those sounds. Take the word 'sour', for instance, which contains a triphthong. It's a combination of **a**, the shorter **oo** and the neutral vowel, which is often represented in dictionaries as an upsidedown **e**, and encountered in such words as 'c(o)ntain', '(a)bout' 'Asc(o)t'.

Or look at 'pliers'. It contains **a** (as in 'bad'), **i** (as in 'bid') and the neutral vowel. 'Air' contains **e** (bed) and the neutral vowel for that slight change of direction at the end.

Look now at the following words and see if you can decide whether they contain pure vowels, diphthongs or triphthongs, but don't look at the answers below yet.

1. tube
2. pew
3. toy
4. noise
5. wire
6. weir

7. room
8. plead
9. coach
10. leer

And these are the answers:

1. diphthong (Vowel Scale lines 2 and 9)
2. diphthong (2 and 9 again)
3. diphthong (6 and 2)
4. diphthong (6 and 2)
5. triphthong (4, 2 and 10)
6. diphthong (2 and 10)
7. pure (9)
8. pure (1)
9. diphthong (6 and 8)
10. diphthong (2 and 10)

Where we see consonants and vowels vying for attention is when we mouth the w sound. Do it now. The lips form a small *round* o. Before you relax your lips, ask yourself this: have you just said 'moo' or are you about to say 'wind'?

We'll do some exercises now for agility of the tongue, lips and jaw. Say the following words very slowly, noticing the 'change of direction' within the vowel sound, and exaggerate the muscular movements, while placing in memory the position of the mouth in achieving the particular vowel sound.

POWER	PAYER	PIER
BOY	BAY	BYRE
CREATE	LIAISE	REINSTATE
PURE	CURE	SURE
HOUR	FLOUR	BOWER
SEWER	DOER	MOOR

Notice that, even with words that look as though they may be exactly similar in vowel sounds, there are subtle differences. The last three, for instance, don't use the same vowel sounds, but they're very close. There's a decreasing emphasis on the **w** sound in the middle of each word, 'sewer' being the strongest in this respect. Some people's vowels may not be as clear as they should, and this will give rise to indistinct speech. Try the 'you what?' test. Try to remember, during the course of five minutes' conversation, how many times your listener has to say 'you what?' (or perhaps more politely, 'I beg your pardon?').

So let's now continue the exercises. And a word of warning here: you'll have to gauge for yourself just how vigorous you'll be able to be with these exercises, in case you damage the fraenum — the small fold of skin under the tongue. If you stick your tongue out too far, for instance, it could be painful, so work up gradually to the maximum agility.

Start by opening your mouth so the teeth are about three-quarters of an inch (or two centimetres) wide, and allow the tongue to rest behind the bottom teeth. Say **EE** and then **AH** alternately. Stand in front of a mirror to do this, and watch what your tongue is doing as it changes from the position needed to create one vowel to the position for the other.

You'll notice that the main body of the tongue (the centre, as it's called) is rising for **EE** and falling for **AH**. Repeat this movement — with or without vocalisation — for a few moments until the tongue feels slightly tired. (The tongue should have already been exercised in other ways during the chapter on consonants, so this shouldn't present too much difficulty for you!)

Now open the mouth as wide as is comfortable and stick the tongue out, moving it first up and down and then from side to side in quick succession.

THE RESONATOR SCALE

Now, as you give yourself a rest from this vigorous exercise, let's consider another phenomenon of speech that adds to the final result. If you whisper **OO** and **EE**, you'll be aware of a note — not a note formed by the voice, but by air pushing through the respective spaces you've created. **OO** is far lower than **EE**. We can go from the lowest to the highest in this order:

OO, u, OH, AW, o, AH, u, ER, a, e, AY, i, EE

Remember it like this: 'Do put whole thought on art, thus turn sad men gay with zeal.'

If you place your mouth into the position for saying **OO**, but instead say the word 'appeal', you'll hear a hollowness to the vowel sound. You'll notice this tendency — although not as exaggerated — in some regional speakers, and this all adds to that final product we think of as their accent.

All this serves to illustrate just how interrelated our components of speech are.

Finally, let's go through a few jingles, one for each of the 24 vowel sounds, mouthing each one deliberately, feeling where the areas of the mouth are placed for each one.

For **EE**:   **Sleazy Peter squealed to see the sequel.**

For **i**:   **Clint spit the pip into the bin.**

For **e**:   **Teddy Redneck kept lead at the head of his bed.**

For **a**:   **The fat man with the hat was happy.**

For **AH**:   **Aunt Martha danced and pranced.**
            (This assumes RP.)

For o: Not a lot to tot up in October.

For AW: Autumn causes awesome Audrey's
                 haughty daughter to become naughty
                 rather than sporty.

For oo: Don't cook the books like a crook.

For OO: Stoop to the fool on the mule.

For u: Come, Constable, hurry.

For ER: The early bird catches the worm.

For OH: Oh, no, the road is closed.

For AY: I say, May, did it rain today?

For I: I sighed as I tried to hide.

For OW: How now! The brown cow had a row
                 with a stout round sow.

For OI: What noise annoys an oyster? A noisy
                 noise annoys an oyster.

For EW: There were few in the queue to get a
                 view as the beautiful curlew flew.

For AIR: The air became rarefied where Mary
                 went spare.

For OOR: The poor amour fell into the Ruhr.

For EAR: Steer clear of the racketeer, dear.

For **URE:**   **The allure of a cure made his aches
                 seem fewer.**

For **OUR:**   **Don't cower in our bower on the hour,
                 my flower.**

For **IRE:**   **I admire your attire entirely, squire.**

Now try some exercises for separating similar sounds, such as the **oo** in 'bull' and the **u** in 'cup' (again, I'm assuming RP here, because in some northern counties the **oo** and **u** sounds would be the same).

**It was an uphill struggle to push the bull the full
way to Solihull. (u and oo)**

A cupful of sugar. (u and oo)

**Consider the content awhile. (Notice the neutral
vowel in 'consider', but o has its full value in 'content';
'connect' and 'continue' would use the neutral, but
'contest' and 'conflict' (as nouns) wouldn't.)**

**He gasped as his past flashed rapidly before his
eyes. (a and AH: here Received Pronunciation would
lengthen 'gasped' and 'past', and 'flashed' and
'rapidly' would have the short a: however, the
Yorkshire or Lancashire speaker, for instance, would
use a short a for the lot.)**

**Russ showed disgraceful behaviour up on the top
deck of the full bus. What a fuss! (u and oo)**

In the next chapter you'll use your newfound awareness and muscular agility to cope with Laura ...

4.

LAURA AND HER FRIENDS
A few common errors and how to eliminate them

If you value good speech, you'll cringe when you hear people speak of our old friend Miss Norder. Laura to her friends. Yes, that's the one — Laura Norder.

In this chapter we'll be looking at a few common speech faults, such as putting an **r** where it shouldn't be — as in the example above — weakness or over sibilance of the **s**, the glottal stop, the uvular **r** and one or two more.

Let's look at Laura first. The **r** does tend to creep in where it's not wanted, and this usually happens when one word ends with a vowel, and the next word begins with one. So there's a tendency to stick an **r** between 'law' and 'order', or in the middle of 'idea of'.

There's a journalist I often hear on Radio Four, who used to be on the independent radio network, who made me think her name was quite different because of this habit. I won't give you her actual name, but a similar one that illustrates the point. Her sign-off when she'd presented a voice report during a news bulletin would be, 'Anna Ratkins, IRN, London'. I thought it rather unfortunate for the poor woman to have to live with a name like Ratkins, when I realised that it wasn't Ratkins at all, but Atkins.

It takes some practice to eliminate this and, it must be said, that when it's used moderately it doesn't sound *that* bad. But you should try to eliminate it if you can, and at the very least you'll be left with only a suggestion of it.

However, once you're out of that particular frying pan, there's the inevitable fire, I'm afraid. Because the tendency then is to use a glottal stop instead.

This was explained more fully in Chapter Two. It's formed when the vocal cords come together, trapping air for a second before releasing it in a small explosion. Using an exclamation mark for the glottal stop, we could make a typical sentence look like this:

Did !Anna !Atkins !ever !eat the !other !apple?

And, although it's permissible to pronounce a linking **r** when it's there — and, indeed, handy as a transitional consonant, as in 'ever eat' — many people are quite happy to let the glottal stop rush in like air into a vacuum whenever they're in doubt. Another speech fault, not quite as common, is the uvular **r** — the one that's overpronounced by English people doing stagy French accents. The tendency here is to form the **r** at the uvula — that small, fleshy, conical stalactite that dangles from the soft palate at the back of the mouth. The enunciation point for the **r** should, of course, be further forward.

Then there's that old favourite, used all over Britain but mostly among Londoners, and that's the substitution of a **v** or **f** for the voiced and unvoiced **th**. One thinks of the phrase, 'Forty fahzand fevvers on a frush's froat.'

THE ANATOMY OF THE MOUTH

We've already seen what happens in the mouth when certain sounds are formed. This section will enlarge on that. A thorough awareness of where everything is and what it does in relation to everything else will help greatly in making muscular adjustments necessary for correcting speech faults.

The very tip of the tongue is called just that: the tip. Behind it is the blade. Behind that is the front and behind that is the centre. This is the main body of the tongue, the part that rises and falls when we speak **EE** and **AH**. Behind that is the back of the tongue, the part that comes into contact with the soft palate, or velum, for forming **ng**, **k** and the hard **g**.

You'll remember from Chapter Two that the tip of the tongue comes into contact with the alveolar ridge for **t**. And that the hard palate is above the centre of the tongue, and the soft palate is above the back of the tongue.

DIFFICULTIES WITH S

Several difficulties are associated with **s**. One common problem is a weak **s** caused by a tendency to use **th**. Another is the over-sibilant **s**, caused by having the tongue too far back along the alveolar ridge. First, you must find the combination of positions that forms the **s**:

1. Place the tip of the tongue against the back of the top teeth to say **th**.

2. Having taken enough breath to sound a sustained, *un*voiced **th**, do so and gradually move the tip of the tongue back, first to the top of the teeth, then onto the alveolar ridge and even further back so that it begins to curl along the hard palate.

3. Keep monitoring the positions and the corresponding sounds. During that movement you should have heard **th** change into a thin **s** into a more 'whistly' **s** and then into **r**. If you were vocalising,

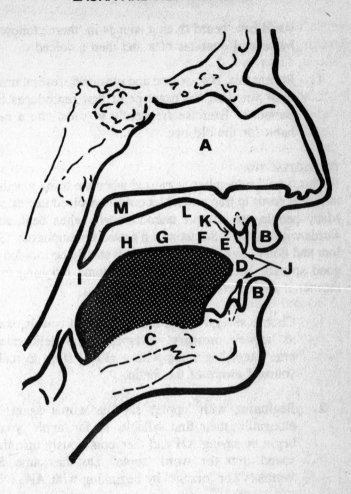

Parts of the mouth and head that contribute to speech.

A	Nasal cavity	H	Back
B	Lips	I	Uvula
C	Tongue	J	Teeth
D	Tip	K	Alveolar ridge
E	Blade	L	Hard palate
F	Front	M	Soft palate (velum)
G	Centre		

you'd have heard **th** as it sounds in 'there', followed by several qualities of **z** and then a voiced **r**.

4 . Repeat this, both voiced and unvoiced, several times until you find the exact point that reproduces the perfect **s**. Exercise frequently to substitute a new habit for the old one.

THE GLOTTAL STOP

This, you'll remember, is caused when we bring together the vocal cords to trap air and let out an unvoiced explosion. Many people use it quite unconsciously when beginning words with a vowel. Sometimes it's used for emphasis: 'Get !*out* and don't !*ever* come back.' But it should be avoided in good speech, because it can soon become irritating to a listener if over used.

1 . Choose several words that begin with vowels, such as 'apple', 'ordinary', 'everyday', and deliberately utter them beginning with a glottal stop, to make yourself aware of the feeling.

2 . Beginning with 'apple', say the words again by elongating their first syllable: so for 'apple' you'll begin by saying **AH** and then consciously turn that sound into the word 'apple'. Do the same for 'ordinary' or 'orange' by beginning with **AW**.

3 . Get used to that feeling of having the word begin without that glottal stop, and, as it were, jot down the sensation on your memory.

4 . Try another approach, just to reinforce the previous one. Place your lips as if to say **m**, but actually stop short of doing so, and without moving anything else

in your mouth or throat, open the lips and say 'apple', 'ordinary', 'everyday', and so on.

What you're doing is bringing the energy to the front of the mouth and away from the glottis, where it can do harm. But, having decided not to pronounce the **m**, you should end up with a perfect vowel. You'll soon get the feeling of how the word is supposed to sound. Now this is all very fine when we're mouthing the word in isolation, you'll say. Quite right. It's far more difficult to think about this when we're in full flow in front of an audience, whether that be of one or many.

So practice is important, and it's only by frequent and consciously applied practice that you can substitute new habits for old.

But you can extend the exercise above by taking some phrases. Let's take our old friend Anna Atkins for starters. The **a** at the end of 'Anna' is, anyway, a neutral vowel, so you'll notice that the vowel sound has to turn a corner as the word 'Atkins' begins. This will allow you to differentiate between the two **a**s.

Now say, 'The idea of it!' The tendency is to use a glottal stop or an intrusive **r**. Practise changing direction between the end of 'idea' and beginning of 'of' while resisting the temptation to use a glottal stop or an intrusive **r**.

Say **AH** followed quickly by **AW** and feel the change of vowel direction without a glottal stop or intrusive **r**. Repeat this several times, **AH-AW-AH-AW**.

Another way of increasing your awareness of how it *should* feel is to begin uttering a syllable in whispers, and gradually vocalise. Start with **AH**. Take a good breath, whisper **AAAH**, without a rasping sound, and gradually introduce vocalisation.

You'll be aware of the vocal cords coming together to begin the vocalisation, and to introduce a glottal stop there would present you with a very obvious feeling of choking back the word.

The glottal stop appears elsewhere, of course. Often it takes the place of t in words such as 'butter', which becomes 'bu!!er'. You'll also hear it coming after a vowel but before a consonant, for instance, 'thir!teen' and 'four!teen'. In the former instance, there's no substitute for good old-fashioned practice. Be aware of when you're saying it, become conscious of it, correct it.

In the latter case, imagine that the first syllable ends with the t, rather than thinking of the second syllable *beginning* with it: THIRT-EEN, FOURT-EEN.

Practise by splitting the words up into their syllables and speaking them slowly and deliberately at first, and then, having become accustomed to omitting the glottal stop, articulate the word as you would in conversation.

Never feel self-conscious about any slight defect you may have, or feel you have, in your speech. Remember that speech is so much taken for granted that such things never usually enter our minds. Our learning of it in infancy was an imitative act and not something we spoke about in terms of alveolar ridges and soft palates. This is why we need to 'feel' our way around. So satisfy yourself that you're fully aware of what's happening at every stage before moving on to the next.

THE INTRUSIVE R

This intrudes in much the same way as the glottal stop. Miss Norder and Miss Ratkins aren't too aware of it, but you are, now that you've been practising.

In Laura's case we can rid ourselves of the intrusive r by remembering that the phrase 'law and order' gives us a perfect device for the transition from 'law' to 'and', and that's the w. It shouldn't be overpronounced, of course, but it's perfectly acceptable to use it to link the two words.

In Anna's case, it's not so easy, but using the method we looked at above for the glottal stop should enable you to move easily from one word to another without making it sound like one long vowel.

Use a taperecorder or an understanding friend. Listen to yourself and professional speakers such as accomplished newsreaders.

On the occasions when there *is* an **r**, of course, it's perfectly permissible to use it as a link: 'heir apparent', 'for instance', 'Rear Admiral'.

Try the following:

In the interests of law and order, Anna Atkins asked the heir apparent about the Rear Admiral's idea of his own authority.

In April, Edmund and I are happy to wander over to the edge of the ornate arbour.

THE UVULAR R

Some notable speakers have got away with using the uvular **r** throughout their careers; some have even made a feature of it. It's often confused with a similar speech fault that substitutes a **w** for an **r**, so we'll attempt to address them both in this section.

The w-for-r is a more obvious substitution, and takes little explanation: we saw how the **w** was formed in Chapter Two. But you may not immediately know what's happening when a uvular **r** is uttered.

The uvula, as we learned earlier, is the dangly bit of flesh at the back of the throat. Anything pertaining to this area is usually referred to as 'uvular'.

Earlier I used the phrase 'enunciation point' to describe exactly where a consonant is made. For the **k**, for instance, it's at the back of the mouth. The uvular **r** starts life there, too, although in this case the throat is partly open.

For the **r** as it's conventionally spoken, the enunciation point is just behind the alveolar ridge, so that's where you should now concentrate your attention if you have difficulty with *your* **r**s.

1. First say **t**, and then change it to **s**. Now let the tongue continue its journey, curling back until the sibilance stops. You should have an **r**.

2. Now try it from the position for **l**. Again, curl the tongue back until you have an **r**.

3. Say the following, feeling the tongue moving back and curling: SHRUG, SHREW, SRI LANKA; THROW; THREW; TRIP, TREE, TROD, TROWBRIDGE; PRAY, PROW, PRURIENT; jot down the sensation on the memory. Practise often if you have difficulty with **r**.

I'll end with something that isn't a fault, but many people mistakenly think it is. Often, two words come together, and the consonant at the end of the first is the same as or similar to the first letter of the second word: 'bad day', 'part time', 'soft touch', 'hard times', 'sit down'. Some people, thinking it slovenly to do otherwise, will give full value to both **t**s in 'part time' or the **d** and the **t** in 'hard times'. It's perfectly acceptable not to do so, but to hang onto the consonant for marginally longer than you would if you were speaking only one of those words. This is sometimes called 'incomplete plosion'.

Even when the consonants are less similar, as with 'back door', there's no need to overdo the **k** and make it sound like 'back-a-door'; but if the **k** were the last letter of your phrase it would be given more value.

Another common fault is to think it wrong to use elision

— that is, missing part of a word out for the sake of articulation. We've already looked at contractions such as 'I've' and 'we'd'. Another is the dropping of the h in 'may have'. It's perfectly acceptable to say 'may've' even if you're reading from a text that says 'may have', because it helps the flow.

Another acceptable form of elision is the **d** in 'and', as it occurs in such phrases as 'town and country'.

Try an experiment. Take a piece of text and deliberately pronounce all the consonants (unless, of course, they're the silent type, such as the **g** in 'night'). Your reading will sound affected. Now read the piece again as you would say it in conversation, and mark the consonants you left out.

If in doubt, you can't go far wrong by listening to good newsreaders on radio and television. Many of them have trained voices and an acute awareness of the requirements of good speech.

5.

TUNING UP
The music of the voice

If, as we saw earlier, vowels are the building blocks of speech and consonants are the mortar, then we can extend the analogy and think of the music of the voice, its expressiveness, as the architecture.

A voice that remains on or around one note is a dull voice indeed, but it's the fate of us all, unfortunately, to hear such voices in our everyday dealings with the world. Even some professional speakers such as lecturers will drone on without a thought for vocal music. Their listeners all too often mentally turn off.

There are various ways to approach expressiveness, and we must employ all of them if our voices are to be interesting and lively. Differing pitch is one; another is varying volume and yet another is our ability to pause and point words. There's the amount of attack we give to our consonants, and there's the pace at which we speak.

INCREASING PITCH

Let's look at pitch first. Many of us don't employ our full vocal range when speaking; others overdo it, as though they were speaking to a baby. Some maintain a pitch that's too high, and others will remain in the lower registers, perhaps believing that it makes them sound more authoritative.

By far the most common of these is a reluctance to use the full range of our voice. Singing is a good antidote. It doesn't matter if you don't sing well. Either choose a song with good range, or do some scale exercises using the tonic sol-fa, beginning on a low note and singing 'do, re, mi' and so on until you reach top **do**, and then going further until you *begin* to strain. It's important not to go too far too quickly, or you could do damage to your voice.

Having thus sung the tonic sol-fa, choose bottom **do, mi, so** and top **do**, singing 'do, mi, so, do, so, mi, do', in rising then falling pitch.

Using the same four-note tune, going up and then back down, sing the words, 'I'm going up, coming down, going up, coming down …' and so on. Then, take the second note up, **mi**, and use that as **do**. You've performed what a musician calls a modulation, an upward shift in key, by two full tones. Do the same again, raising the pitch value of **do**, until you've fully tested your range, and become aware of the muscular sensations that accompany finding new notes, both low and high. I've deliberately avoided using the musical five-line stave filled with blobs, because I for one don't fully understand written music and I should hate to confuse others who similarly find it a blind spot.

Now speak the following jingle, doing what it says:

I'm speaking low, so very low,
But now a little higher I go;
And higher still until I strain,
And now I start back down again —
Slowly does it with a slide
As back down to the bass I glide.

If you don't feel too self-conscious about it, say it into a taperecorder and listen. It's so often necessary to remind ourselves from time to time just how we sound, because we invariably don't sound the same to ourselves as we do to others. In my work as a broadcaster in independent radio, I still, after a dozen years in the business, set a taperecorder to catch the odd broadcast, and listen back for any speech faults that need some attention.

Now look at this sentence: 'Did Martha give you the book yesterday?' There are as many possible meanings in that sentence as there are words in it, and we point up the differences by the simple use of pitch and volume.

'*Did* Martha give you the book yesterday?' asks if she really did give it to you.

'Did *Martha* give you the book yesterday?' questions whether it was Martha or someone else.

'Did Martha *give* you the book yesterday?' asks whether she gave it to you or perhaps sold it to you.

'Did Martha give *you* the book yesterday?' asks whether it was you she gave it to and not someone else.

'Did Martha give you *the* book yesterday?' suggests that it's a very special book you're talking about, and not just any old book.

'Did Martha give you the *book* yesterday?' implies that perhaps it wasn't the book she gave you, but something else.

And 'Did Martha give you the book *yesterday*?' questions whether it was yesterday or today or some other day.

We don't usually have any difficulty knowing which word to emphasise when we're in full flow in everyday speech, yet it's surprising how many people fail to do so when they're reading a prepared text, such as a speech or a news bulletin or a report at a staff or management meeting.

And, even if we *do* know which words to stress, not everyone stresses them quite enough to inject vitality into their sentences.

So here's an exercise to perform with a friend. Give her a copy of the list of 'Martha' sentences, while you have your own copy. Choose one of the variations at random and don't speak but *hum* the sentence to your friend, and ask her to identify which one you were looking at.

Then, take this principle a stage further, and type or write out two copies of some different sentences from a book or newspaper, and ask your friend to do the honours once more. But this time they won't be variations of the same sentence, so this should really tax your expressiveness.

It always pays to exaggerate the stresses at first, and then, if you feel that you're a bit over the top, bring it down to an acceptable level. After you've done some practice in this way, *always* take some text and do some reading aloud. If you followed my suggestion in the introduction, you'll already be reading aloud from *this* book whenever you can.

POINTING AND PAUSING

To point a word is simply to highlight it. Stress, discussed above, is just one method of pointing. Pausing is another — either before or after the word you wish to point, or, indeed, both before and after. Look at this extract from Lincoln's Gettysburg speech:

It is rather for us to be here dedicated to the great task remaining before us; that from these honoured dead we take increased devotion to that cause for which they gave the last full measure of devotion; that we here highly resolve that these dead shall

not have died in vain; that this nation, under God, shall have a new birth of freedom; and that government of the people, by the people and for the people shall not perish from the earth.

Stirring stuff, you'll agree. Now that could be said with few pauses and few stresses, but would sound quite dull, and the delivery wouldn't be doing justice to the noble words and sentiments.

So read it aloud and put pauses where you think they might add to expressiveness. I've reproduced the excerpt below with my own interpretation, but don't worry too much if yours and mine don't coincide — there's no definitive interpretation.

It is rather for us to be here// dedicated to the great task remaining before us;// that from these honoured dead// we take increased devotion to that cause// for which they gave the last// full measure of devotion;// that we here// highly resolve// that these dead// shall not have died in vain;// that this nation, under God,// shall have a new birth of freedom;// and that government// of the people,// by the people// and for the people// shall not perish from the earth.

If, in your mind's ear, you listen to the words of Lincoln being addressed to a large gathering, you can see that the pauses are effective for dramatic purposes as well as to cope with the size of the space. The same words delivered to a cosy little group sitting in a circle wouldn't require that type of delivery — but it's highly unlikely that those words would be chosen for a small cosy group, anyway.

Now look at this short extract from a famous Winston Churchill speech:

> **Let us therefore brace ourselves to our duties, and so bear ourselves that, if the British Empire and its Commonwealth last for a thousand years, men will still say this was their finest hour.**

It rather defies you not to pause both before and after the word 'this' doesn't it? But consider now the *length* of the pause. Personally, I would put half a beat before the word, and a full beat after it. I would also further point 'this' with an increase in volume. Try it different ways and experiment.

There's no definitive way, and each piece of text will require its own delivery. But be aware of the power of the pause. In everyday informal speech it may sound just a little affected to keep pausing for effect, but just about all of us at some time are called upon to 'say a few words' at a retirement presentation or a wedding or other social occasion. As you rehearse your speech, you'll soon remember where to put the pauses. If you're going to read it from a script, you can mark the pauses, of course, so you'll have a visual prompt.

(*Reading* a speech is not always a good idea, but we'll discuss this further in Chapter Nine.)

VOWEL LENGTH

Say 'enormous' quickly, and then say it with a ridiculously exaggerated vowel length in the second syllable. It has the effect of making the word much bigger, matching delivery and meaning. Experiment with vowel length on several words — even as you read these — and listen for the differences in the power of the word.

Again, there's no one way, no exact vowel length. You need to experiment, to evaluate the word you're about to read or say. It should become automatic, as your awareness of words becomes more and more apparent to you, and with it an appreciation of the extra layers of meaning that are possible with good delivery.

Working with verse is, I believe, the most useful method of gaining greater flexibility. Poetry makes words work quite differently from prose: it can be extravagant, and allows you, the reader, to be extravagant, too, without being unfaithful to the meaning in the text.

Metrical verse is better, but you should also choose some free verse and look for the possibilities it presents for squeezing the last ounce of meaning out of each word.

Don't worry if you have no intention of ever reciting verse in public, or even of making a small speech, because thinking about words in this way will add to your subconscious awareness of your delivery, and you should begin to notice improvements in your everyday speech behind the counter, on the telephone, in the office or with friends, as well as finding the process of speech much more interesting.

We'll look at some verses now for practice, beginning with two from Lewis Carroll, the first from *Alice's Adventures in Wonderland*, and the second from *Through the Looking-Glass*.

> 'Will you walk a little faster?' said a whiting to a
>   snail,
> 'There's a porpoise close behind us, and he's
>   treading on my tail.
> See how eagerly the lobsters and the turtles all
>   advance!
> They are waiting on the shingle — will you come
>   and join the dance?
> Will you, won't you, will you, won't you, will
>   you join the dance?
> Will you, won't you, will you, won't you, won't
>   you join the dance?
>
> 'You can really have no notion how delightful it
>   will be

When they take us up and throw us, with the
    lobsters, out to sea!'
But the snail replied, 'Too far, too far!' and gave
    a look askance —
Said he thanked the whiting kindly, but he would
    not join the dance.
Would not, could not, would not, could not,
    would not join the dance;
Would not, could not, would not, could not,
    could not join the dance.

'What matters it how far we go?' his scaly friend
    replied.
'There is another shore, you know, upon the
    other side.
The further off from England, the nearer is to
    France —
Then turn not pale, beloved snail, but come and
    join the dance.
Will you, won't you, will you, won't you, will
    you join the dance?
Will you, won't you, will you, won't you, won't
    you join the dance?'

Then there's the famous *Jabberwocky*, which is great fun
to read and gives you the opportunity to use nonsense words
as though they were part of everyday speech.

'Twas brillig, and the slithy toves
Did gyre and gimble in the wabe;
All mimsy were the borogoves,
And the mome raths outgrabe.

'Beware the Jabberwock, my son!
The jaws that bite, the claws that catch!

Beware the Jubjub bird, and shun
The frumious Bandersnatch!'

He took his vorpal sword in hand;
Long time the manxome foe he sought —
So rested he by the Tumtum tree,
And stood awhile in thought.

And, as in uffish thought he stood,
The Jabberwock, with eyes of flame,
Came whiffling through the tulgey wood,
And burbled as it came!

One, two! One, two! And through and through
The vorpal blade went snicker-snack!
He left it dead, and with its head
He went galumphing back.

'And hast thou slain the Jabberwock?
Come to my arms, my beamish boy!
O frabjous day! Callooh! Callay!'
He chortled in his joy.

'Twas brillig, and the slithy toves
Did gyre and gimble in the wabe;
All mimsy were the borogoves,
And the mome raths outgrabe.

At first, exaggerate all the consonants and vowels, and
feel the muscle sensations required. Then examine each
word for its potential, and mark it lightly in pencil for the
way you intend to treat it (or copy out the verses if you
prefer not to mark your book).

Now we'll look at a famous Rupert Brooke poem called
The Great Lover. I've chosen this one because there's such

a long list of things he loves that you'll be hard-pressed to give each one its verbal value. Watch for the punctuation, as this will help you to evaluate each phrase, and know where to pause to gather energy for the next item or group of items. Here we go:

These I have loved:
White plates and cups, clean-gleaming,
Ringed with blue lines; and feathery, faery dust;
Wet roofs, beneath the lamplight; the strong
   crust
Of friendly bread; and many-tasting food;
Rainbows; and the blue bitter smoke of wood;
And radiant raindrops couching in cool flowers;
And flowers themselves, that sway through sunny
   hours,
Dreaming of moths that drink them under the
   moon;
Then, the cool kindliness of sheets, that soon
Smooth away trouble; and the rough male kiss
Of blankets; grainy wood; live hair that is
Shining and free; blue-massing clouds; the keen
Unpassioned beauty of a great machine;
The benison of hot water; furs to touch;
The good smell of old clothes; and other such —
The comfortable smell of friendly fingers;
Hair's fragrance; and the musty reek that lingers
About dead leaves and last year's ferns ...

Dear names,
And thousand others throng to me! Royal flames;
Sweet water's dimpling laugh from tap or spring;
Holes in the ground; and voices that do sing;
Voices in laughter, too; and body's pain,
Soon turned to peace; and the deep-panting train;

Firm sands; the little dulling edge of foam
That browns and dwindles as the wave goes
      home;
And washen stones, gay for an hour; the cold
Graveness of iron; moist black earthen mould;
Sleep; and high places; footprints in the dew;
And oaks; and brown horse-chestnuts,
      glossy-new;
And new-peeled sticks; and shining pools on
      grass; —
All these have been my loves.

In the Brooke piece we encounter some of the gentler,
almost wistful emotional responses we feel when we're
being nostalgic. In the next poem, the emotions are much
stronger, and I want you to use the power of the words to
excite the emotions within you, thus charging your own
delivery with the emotion Wilfred Owen intended his
readers to feel, and no doubt himself felt when he thought
bitterly of the futility, the obscenity, of war. (The Latin at
the end, by the way, is sometimes seen on war memorials.
It means 'It is sweet and fitting to die for one's country.')

Bent double, like old beggars under sacks,
Knock-kneed, coughing like hags, we cursed
      through sludge,
Till on the haunting flares we turned our backs,
And towards our distant rest began to trudge.
Men marched asleep. Many had lost their boots,
But limped on, blood-shod. All went lame, all
      blind;
Drunk with fatigue; deaf even to the hoots
Of gas-shells dropping softly behind.

**Gas! Gas! Quick, boys! – An ecstasy of
  fumbling,
Fitting the clumsy helmets just in time;
But someone still was yelling out and stumbling
And floundering like a man in fire or lime.
Dim through the misty panes and thick green
  light
As under a green sea, I saw him drowning.**

**In all my dreams before my helpless sight
He plunges at me, guttering, choking, drowning.
If in some smothering dreams, you too could
  pace
Behind the wagon that we flung him in,
And watch the white eyes writhing in his face,
His hanging face, like a devil's sick of sin;
If you could hear, at every jolt, the blood
Come gargling from the froth-corrupted lungs
Bitter as the cud
Of vile, incurable sores on innocent tongues,
My friend, you would not tell with such high zest
To children ardent for some desperate glory,
The old Lie: *Dulce et decorum est
Pro patria mori*.**

Notice how you're tempted to increase the pace in the second stanza after the plodding pace of the first. Consider the three words 'men marched asleep', and how they suggest by their rhythm exactly what they're describing.

It won't fall to you in everyday conversation to choose your words in the way a poet does, but by thinking of words in this way you will soon build up an appreciation that will colour the way you speak.

Think of vowel length, pausing and pointing, pitch and volume. And there's another way of adding to our words, and that's by how hard or soft our consonants are.

Say 'He was bad, very bad' and exaggerate the *b* and *d* each time you say 'bad'. See how emphatic that adjective has become for you. You really wanted to tell your listener just how bad he was, and did so not only by choosing the right descriptive word but by how you chose to utter it.

Try the same with 'She was quite enchanting' and make the **ch** in 'enchanting' just as harsh. Oh, dear! She doesn't sound all *that* enchanting, does she? It makes you sound quite resentful about how enchanting she was, as though she'd done a great wrong by displaying her charms. Say it now with a softer **ch**, and you have it as it was meant.

It's here that we enter the field of verbal dynamics, which is a whole subject in itself. But you can get a feel for it by choosing a word such as 'flung' and performing an action to accompany it. Pick up an imaginary garment, which you're going to fling into a corner. Say the sentence, 'And he *flung* it into the corner', and perform the action of flinging as you utter the word.

You'll probably start a downward and outward movement of the gripped hand with the **fl**, your hand will make its sweep during the short vowel, **u**, and, as you utter **ng**, probably elongating it slightly, you'll let go your grip and see the garment flying cornerwards.

Go back to the Owen poem above, and look at some of the verbs and the phrases they govern.

'Men *marched* asleep …', '… the wagon that we *flung* him in …', 'an ecstasy of *fumbling, fitting* the clumsy helmets …', '… *writhing* in his face …', '… *gargling* from the froth-corrupted lungs …'.

Now similarly examine words such as 'leap', 'blare', 'split', 'crash', 'crunch', 'snap', 'grab' and others that suggest action and sound.

PACE

We touched on pace above when we considered the start
of the second stanza of *Dulce et decorum est*. Listen to the
difference between a cricket commentator and a football
commentator on radio or television. Cricket is by far the
more leisurely game, and this is reflected in the way the
commentator speaks of it. Football, on the other hand,
compresses all of its action into 90 minutes.

Now look for the point in the following passage where
you would change pace:

**Snoozing peacefully on the divan, Eleanor dreamed
of places she had visited as a child — faraway places
that smelled of the sea and spoke of long days
stretching before her excited little-girl's eyes. She
let out a long sigh, half awake now, luxuriating in
the tranquility of the terrace and the sound of the
lapping blue water of the nearby swimming pool.
She had the place to herself for another three
hours. She let that thought wash over her mind
gently. Then she was fully awake. Something had
moved in one of the bushes. Then there was another
movement, and then another. She shot off the divan
and pulled on a bathrobe, looking wildly around
her for the next movement. Again it happened, this
time at the other side of the pool, and then another
movement a few yards further on, as *something*
seemed to be making swift progress through the
thick bushes. Still she could see nothing but the
movement suggested by the swishing leaves. But a
sudden screech left her in no doubt where the
movements were, an ululation that shattered the
peace as surely as a police siren. Eleanor ran,
tripping on the stone step, ran, fell, got up and ran,
unaware of bleeding shins, until she reached the**

house. She slammed the door behind her and shot the bolt, and then leaned against it, panting, regaining her breath and her senses. Eleanor knew that anyone else would have put the strange movements down to an animal — the Alsatian from the house along the road perhaps — but she knew it was no animal.

You could make a case there for speeding up when the noises began, and slowing the pace a little towards the end, when a touch of the sinister is introduced into the narrative.

It shouldn't be too difficult to find short passages in novels or short stories whose pace changes. And soon you'll see how effective a change of pace can make any narrative or speech. There's further good practice to be had, of course, in reading bedtime stories to children.

YOUR VOICE IS YOU

Always bear in mind when thinking of expressiveness that your voice is ultimately an expression of you. If it's all a listener is aware of — such as when you're on the telephone or speaking on local radio — then your voice *is* you. All that we've discussed so far in separate chapters will ultimately be brought together into a complex, interrelated whole, a synthesis of your childhood, your environment, past and current influences upon you, your image of yourself, your need to influence those around you, your mood of the moment, your current state of health and wellbeing and no doubt many other things that contribute to what your listeners interpret as the essential you. All this becomes your own unique way of expressing yourself through speech.

Take some text now — either something of your choosing or an example from Chapter Eight — and read it, having looked again at the headings in this chapter and used them as a checklist. You'll be bringing to the task all that you've learned about consonants, vowels and expressiveness — the mechanics of the voice itself.

In the next two chapters we'll be looking at some of the factors that lie *behind* the production of sound: breathing and relaxation.

6.

A BREATH OF FRESH AIR
Good breathing leads to good speaking

Being able to control the breath is of vital importance in good speech production. That means not only the amount of air taken into the lungs, but also the rate at which it's let out. This is what's known as breath control.

Listen to some people speak, and count the number of times they pause in the most inappropriate places for a breath. It matters less in conversational speech, but we're back to that very real probability that one day you're going to be called upon to 'say a few words'.

Good breathing habits make us much freer in our speech, and also contribute to our health generally.

Acquiring the habit of taking in more air all the time must be our first aim. Aim to breathe into the belly. We know that air doesn't really go there, but into our lungs. But it does no harm to imagine that the air's reaching down to our lower abdomen and expanding it.

What's really happening is that the diaphragm — that dome-shaped piece of muscular, membranous tissue that separates the thorax, or chest area, from the abdomen — is moving downwards to accommodate the expansion of the chest.

Between them, the diaphragm and the intercostal

muscles, which are between the ribs, expand the chest, and therefore the lungs, in order to suck in air. The lungs aren't themselves muscles.

As the diaphragm lowers, the middle and lower ribs tend to move outwards. You can prove this by placing the backs of your hands on your lower ribs, first at the front and then behind, and take a deep breath into the abdomen.

The health-giving advantages of maintaining deep breathing throughout everyday life are two-fold:

(a) We need plenty of oxygen to feed our blood, which carries it to other parts of the body, including the brain; and

(b) The action of the diaphragm moving downwards tends to massage the organs in the abdomen, which contributes to their own health and wellbeing.

And, while the primary purpose of breathing is to take oxygen through the body for our very survival, it is also necessary for speech.

Air is the motive force of speech. Without air there could be no speech as we know it. We saw in Chapter One what happens to the air as it ascends from the lungs. Now you need to be aware of how advantageous it is to have *plenty* of that air there in reserve, ready to tackle any vocal task.

So begin now by cultivating the habit of breathing evenly and steadily, and − unless you're already doing this − a good deal more deeply than you may have been used to. Deep, steady breathing also has the advantage of making us feel more relaxed and at ease. Try it for just a moment. Breathe in through the nose to the count of six seconds, hold for four, and then breathe out through the mouth to six. Do that six times, and notice how much more relaxed you feel.

Once you've become accustomed to deeper breathing,

turn your attention to the amount of air you're breathing *out*. Toxins build up in air that's left in the lungs to stagnate. Try to expel as much air as is comfortable for you.

Good breathing exercise can come with walking or running. During the days when I used to do a lot of cross-country runs I took the advice of my old PE teacher and breathed in to so many steps and out to so many steps. During particularly gruelling parts of the course, when more breath was required, I would reduce the number of steps for inhalation and exhalation, and then reinstate the original pattern once I was on the flat again.

When walking, find a pace that's comfortable for you, and regulate your breathing: in to six steps, hold for four, out to four; in to six, hold for four, out to four, and so on. If this is either uncomfortable or too easy, then change the ratio of steps to breath.

INCREASING YOUR LUNG CAPACITY

It's never a bad idea to begin the day as you mean to go on — breathing well, breathing healthily. Air is free (for the time being, at least); enjoy it.

Before you get into restrictive clothes, just stand with your arms loosely by your sides and breathe in steadily. Don't count at this stage: just get used to nice steady breathing. Enjoy the sensation.

Now breathe in to the count of six, and as you do so raise your arms above your head. Hold them there as you hold your breath for four, and then breathe out steadily over six beats, bringing your hands to your chest. Repeat the process, but this time extend your arms out to your sides. As you breathe out, bring them back to the chest, and extend them upwards again to the next inhalation.

Do this for a few moments and feel that your lungs are enjoying being stretched.

Don't feel that you *have* to do this first thing in the

morning, but you'll feel the benefits if you do. And don't think that, because you started your day with breathing exercises, that lets you off for the rest of the day. It doesn't. Try them anywhere you won't feel self-conscious — even nipping to the loo halfway through the morning.

Breathing exercises without the arm movements can be done any time without embarrassment, of course, because no one else will be aware of what you're doing.

And don't forget: you're breathing right down into the belly. The opposite of this deep abdominal breathing is called clavicular breathing, or breathing too high in the chest. Actors may employ this technique deliberately when wanting to give the impression of being breathless.

A word of warning may be appropriate here. Although you'll gradually find that breathing more deeply becomes habitual, at first you may experience moments of light-headedness as you push yourself a little further each time. So don't perform breathing exercises while driving or operating machinery. Be aware of your breathing at these times, by all means, and aim for a steady, controlled and *fairly* full intake of breath, but don't push it.

CONTROLLING THE OUTFLOW

The breath should be controlled by muscular action, and not by trapping it. When breathing in, this doesn't apply. But when you wish to breathe out very slowly you may be aware of holding it in the glottis or by closing the throat. This is not breath control. It's cheating, and doesn't do any good.

Take a breath now, and hold onto it for a few seconds by muscular power alone. The back of the throat and the glottis should remain open and free, and should feel no different when you begin to let the breath out.

Now let it out, slowly and evenly through the mouth, using only the power of your diaphragm and intercostals to keep it from rushing out in a sudden gush.

If you find it difficult to locate and focus upon the sensations in chest and throat, let your voice help. Take a deep breath and hum out on one note for a count of 10 seconds. Any tendency to trap the air in the glottis or throat will now show in the sound, giving it a strained quality.

When you've practised at 10 seconds, try 15, 17 and 20.

In the course of giving a talk or reading a passage from a report, there'll be long sentences and phrases in the middle of which it would be inappropriate to pause. This isn't to say that you should never pause within a sentence; of course you should. Indeed, as we saw in the examples in Chapter Five, it's more than appropriate to do so for the sake of expressiveness. But you shouldn't be having to pause in an *in*appropriate place for want of a full breath.

Now try an experiment. See how far you can go with the following expanding sentence, taking a breath only at the full stops.

* I am.

* I am going.

* I am going to try.

* I am going to try to read.

* I am going to try to read as much as I can.

* I am going to try to read as much as I can of this.

* I am going to try to read as much as I can of this sentence on one breath.

* I am going to try to read as much as I can of this sentence on one breath without gasping.

* I am going to try to read as much as I can of this sentence on one breath without gasping or running out.

* I am going to try to read as much as I can of
  this sentence on one breath without gasping or
  running out of air.

* I am going to try to read as much as I can of
  this sentence on one breath without gasping or
  running out of air or going blue in the face.

You can make things even harder for yourself by choosing
a passage of prose and reading as far as you can,
comfortably, on one breath, obeying the conditions that
were gradually spelled out in the above exercise. Mark the
place you reach and, after some breathing exercises, try
again.

Some teachers of speech say that too much emphasis is
laid on breath capacity. To some extent they're right. We
shouldn't let an ability to hold large lungfuls of breath blind
us to the need for pausing for other reasons. Nor should we
think that, just because we have the air in our lungs to go
on to the next phrase-end, we shouldn't take a breath.
Indeed, we should aim to keep our breath reserve topped up
to a comfortable level at all times.

But our purpose here is to become *aware* of our
breathing, and the freedom good breathing imparts to our
speech.

Now say the following, breathing where you see the
double obliques.

Jack reached the top of the hill, a little breathless
after his exertion.// The climb had made him feel
quite warm,// and he took off his jacket, folded it
down its length, and rested it over his left arm.//
Only then, as he looked around, did the full impact
of the spectacular view of the Yorkshire countryside
hit him.// He took a deep breath, smiled, and began

the journey back to the bottom,// happy to be alive, happy to be here.

You'll notice that there are opportunities there for pausing *for effect*, but not necessarily to take a breath. Read the passage again, breathing at every comma and full stop, and you'll see what I mean. You'll probably end up with too much breath in your lungs by the time you reach the end.

In the end, it's up to you. All I can do is make you aware of the possibilities, and you must then use that new awareness to interpret passages or poems or your own speeches, talks, lectures or conversations, in a way that adds colour and richness to your voice and speech. Sensible breathing will help you to that end.

7.

LETTING GO
The importance of relaxation and confidence

Let's begin with an experiment. Stand comfortably and lift your shoulders up to your ears, so much that you feel uncomfortable. As you hold them there, say, 'Mary had a little lamb ...' Now let them relax and say it again. You should've noticed a distinct difference in the speech quality.

All you did was to exaggerate muscle tension to such a degree that your wind pipe and other accoutrements of speech were constricted.

Believe it or not, many of us are tense throughout much of the day, and even in our sleep. Tension is misdirected energy, and is not only useless but actually causes fatigue and even, in some extreme cases, physical deformities and mental problems.

Stress management is a subject in itself, and many books have been written about it. Stress is a major contributory factor towards muscular tension, and often it's simply a matter of incorrect posture and a lack of awareness of our muscular state at any given time.

And lack of confidence can be a cause of stress when you're about to speak to a gathering. That in turn leads to more stress, which leads to a further feeling of lacking confidence, and you have a vicious circle.

THE RELAXED BODY

But let's look at bodily relaxation first, and then we'll examine some tips on how to attain and *main*tain confidence.

First, let me be clear about what I mean by 'relaxation'. We're not talking here about the total relaxation you feel when in a trance or doing certain yoga exercises. We're talking about the *relative* relaxation found in those parts of the body that aren't active when it's adopting an easy standing or sitting posture.

Focus your attention on your shoulders for a moment. See if they'll drop another inch or so − without forcing them. Many people − myself included − find that this is often the case. Sometimes we need to make a conscious effort to relax, because, quite simply, we don't *know* that we're tense.

But our *body* knows, and that tension is all too easily transmitted to our voice. The shoulders are a case in point. Often, tension goes to the shoulders, neck and other parts of the upper body that are so important for clear, effortless speech.

There are several ways to relax, and we'll be encountering some of them in this chapter. One of them involves lying on the floor. I'm not suggesting you should deliver a speech from that position, unless you're desperate for publicity; but by following the recommended exercises you'll get an idea of the way a relaxed body *should* feel, and commit it to memory.

We'll also touch on posture in this chapter, because good posture will help the process of relaxation and removal of tension. When we speak in a formal or semi-formal situation, our energy should be directed to the act of speech. Energy lurking uselessly elsewhere in the body is energy wasted. This goes for any activity, not just speaking.

Before we do any exercises specifically for relaxation, I

want you to be aware — *acutely* aware — of your body. Stand up, with your feet about 18 inches (or 45 centimetres) apart, holding this book comfortably in one hand so that you can continue reading. Let the other hand rest loosely by your side. If you're reading aloud, as I suggested you should, stop for a few moments and take in the next few instructions silently. This is because I want you to concentrate intently on each part of your body for a moment, directing mental energy to that area and becoming aware of its existence. Yes, we take our bodies so much for granted sometimes that often we see, say, our left foot as something vaguely 'down there' — outside our focus of awareness, which is usually the head.

So think of your feet, and, as you breathe slowly and evenly, let the mental energy you're projecting there come slowly up to the ankles, then the shins and calves, the knees, the thighs, buttocks, pelvic area, abdomen and lower back, chest and upper back, shoulders, upper arms, elbows, forearms, wrists, hands, fingers, then back up the arms again, resting on the shoulders for a moment before going to the neck, lower face, eyes and forehead and scalp.

Quite a list. As your journey progressed, did you notice any particular areas of tension and find yourself making any quick adjustments? I'm not suggesting you *should* have done, but by performing this mental exercise of 'taking stock' every so often you should be able to locate areas where tension gathers.

Before we go on, just note your posture. You should be neither slumped forwards — as this produces tension in the back to compensate — nor arched backwards, as this produces tension in the abdomen and other muscles.

In the last 20 years or so, teachers of speech and voice production have relied more and more on the principles enshrined in the Alexander Technique for correcting postural problems. Frederick Mathias Alexander — an

Australian actor born in 1869 — suffered respiratory problems in childhood, which remained with him until later in life, resulting in a hoarseness that plagued his recitations.

Eventually, Alexander was able to correct this by concentrating intently upon aspects of his lifestyle that many of us take for granted, including the way he stood, sat and walked. He observed himself for months, and noticed that, when he recited, he tended to pull his head back and push it down onto his spine, which tended to depress his larynx.

He noticed that, when he was able to decrease tension in his throat, his hoarseness began to disappear. Teachers of posture often refer to the 'head-neck-back relationship', and tell us that we must always seek to maintain a sense of freedom in that area. Tension, as we learned earlier, tends to congregate there, and it does no harm to become aware of that region every once in a while, and consciously relax it. Soon it'll be second nature to you to *keep* it relaxed.

Alexander referred to the main reflex of the body as the Primary Control, and taught that this was situated in the neck area and governed all other reflexes in the body. As he experimented further with his own posture, he discovered that tension here leads to tension elsewhere in the body.

So it pays us to be vigilant. Are you still standing comfortably, by the way? If you've been adopting a good posture, you shouldn't feel tired by having stood throughout the previous few paragraphs, because your weight should've been so distributed as to obviate the need for any unnecessary tension.

A good posture for speech is to have one foot slightly in front of the other, and the feet at an angle of about 45 degrees. If you allow the weight to bear slightly more on the rear leg than the front, you'll notice that there's less tendency for the hips to be pushed forwards, creating unnecessary tension there.

If you want to go further into the subject of good posture,

there are many books on the subject, including some by Alexander himself.

But, for the moment, suffice it to say that you should aim for an easy posture that allows your weight to be well distributed. You should feel easy. If in doubt, follow the procedure I outlined above, and stand for a while, focusing your attention on the various muscle groups, and 'feeling around' for tension.

EXERCISES FOR RELAXATION

First, those all important shoulders and neck. Feel relaxation by first feeling tension. When you've read the next paragraph, put the book down for a few moments and continue with the exercise.

Stand comfortably. Breathe slowly and evenly. Raise the shoulders to the ears, hold and let go. Note the feeling. Repeat the exercise several times, feeling the difference each time between the extremes of tension and relaxation.

Now the neck. Let the head fall gently forwards, so that your chin wants to touch your chest, but don't force it. (No exercises for relaxation should be forced but, as Hamlet said to his players, 'use all gently'.)

Now let the head roll to the right, hold, now forwards to the chest and to the left. Do that a few times, and then, while your head is to left or right, let it roll back gently and right round to the front. Thus loosened, the head and neck should roll round and round as often as you like, easing that tension away as an iron banishes creases from a shirt.

When standing, feel that the head is well placed on the neck, so there's no tendency for it to fall forwards or backwards. Don't be tempted to thrust the chin forwards, as this will cause tension in the larynx.

An exercise now for more of the body. Reach up and try to touch the ceiling with your fingertips. Feel that the crown of your head is trying to follow your hands. Then let yourself gently fall forwards, so that you're hinged at the waist and your arms are dangling loose (probably with your hands brushing the carpet). Feel a wonderful floppy freedom in all of the upper body. Now, gently raise yourself to a standing position, imagining that the spine is uncurling from the base upwards.

Do this three or more times, to acquaint yourself with that freedom and then lie on the floor, having read the following instructions. Have a couple of paperback books or a thin cushion under your head if this makes you feel more comfortable.

Now an exercise to ease the back. Lie on the floor, arms by your sides a little away from your body, and bend the knees by bringing your heels towards your buttocks. If there's a tendency for the knees to fall apart, move the feet a little further out to each side until your legs find their equilibrium.

Say to yourself silently, 'My back is lengthening and spreading'. Don't try to force it. Mentally check that the whole of the back is touching the floor. Having the knees crooked helps this process.

(Alexander teachers recommend doing this for 20 minutes or so per session, incidentally, using books to support the head, and claims have been made for gains in height as the back is gently urged to correct past mistakes.)

THE CORPSE POSITION

Lie flat, arms by your sides a little away from your body, feet slightly apart. Allow your breathing to steady. Close your eyes and concentrate your attention on your toes. As you breathe in, contract the toe muscles, causing them to tense. As you breathe out, relax them. Feel the difference.

Then tense the whole foot by arching it forwards — breathe in, then relax and breathe out.

Follow the procedure, as you did with the awareness

exercise, right up the body, concentrating on those same muscle groups as you do so, tensing and relaxing. When you reach the face, screw it up as though you'd just drunk a cupful of neat lemon juice. You can tense the scalp by an exaggerated lifting of the eyebrows.

Lie for a few minutes in that position, being aware of each part of your body, and ironing out any tension that may creep back in.

This is the yogi corpse position, but you can modify it by crooking the knees as you did for the back exercise. It's very satisfying to lie like that for a while, and try to empty the mind. If it helps, have some gentle music on the hi-fi as you perform the exercise and just unashamedly enjoy the experience.

When you get up and perhaps go to the kitchen to make coffee or prepare a meal, maybe sit and watch some television or go about your daily work, you should feel the benefit of that exercise. If you do it before going to make your speech or attend that all-important interview, the benefits should carry through with you.

THE RELAXED MIND

This is the other side of relaxation. If the mind is at ease, confidence will win through. Having a relaxed and free body is half the battle. The rest is a combination of ability and attitude.

There are several causes of fear when we go to an interview or to mount a rostrum. One is a feeling that our audience are about to be hostile. This is rarely the case. The audience *want* you to speak; that's why they've turned up to listen. They *want* you to do well and they want to hear your views. This is also the case with the interview. Your potential boss, employee or client is there to listen to what you have to say, and you're there to listen, too.

Another cause is lacking confidence in your ability. But,

if you've paid attention to the factors that make for good speech, then the ability is there. You've already begun giving yourself the ability by buying or borrowing this book.

A third cause is lack of confidence in your material. But, if you've prepared that material well and are sure of (a) your facts and (b) that they're arranged in an accessible order, then that cause is removed. Preparation of your material will form part of the last chapter.

Yet another cause is the fear that you may not be heard. This moves us on to another aspect of good speech: projection.

Projecting isn't shouting. It's about (a) having the vocal capabilities to speak clearly and firmly, and (b) using muscular awareness to ensure that there's enough energy behind your words to send them flying to the back of the hall.

These you've covered in previous chapters, but you can consolidate that knowledge with an exercise specifically aimed at projection.

Lie flat on the floor once more, with your knees bent so your back is spread comfortably. Now take a good breath and hum, very softly, on a note that's comfortable to you. Then increase the volume, but not the pitch of the note — in other words, resist the temptation to rise from *do* to *re* to *mi*. Remember to push from the abdomen, not the chest. Continue with the exercise, taking breaths when necessary, and push the volume as hard as your voice will allow without breaking up.

What you're doing is becoming louder without raising the pitch. (Imagine someone whispering sweet nothings into a loved one's ear, then that same person having a stand-up barney with the said loved one, and the pitch of the voice will, in the second case, be somewhat higher.)

Now, remain on your back, and have some text that

you've prepared − that is, learned by heart. Even our old friend Mary and her little lamb will help, or there may be a favourite poem, piece of prose, words to a song or hymn or even the Lord's Prayer.

Take a good breath as you did for the humming exercise, and speak, first low and soft, then increasing the volume after each breath. Do this until your body remembers what's required of it to produce sound good and loud, with all the desirable music of the voice but without increasing the pitch. It won't be easy at first, but after a while it'll become second nature to you, and you'll find yourself practising the technique − in the *upright* position, of course − in crowded streets, bars, meeting halls or discos when you want to cut through the surrounding din.

Don't be tempted, as some people are, to restrict the throat in such a way that the voice comes out strident. It may cut through surrounding noise, but its quality is altogether harsh and unpleasant.

A very useful ploy to adopt when trying to project is imagination. If you mentally aim for a person on the back row, and speak your words as though to that person, they'll have a habit of getting there. Also, push gently with your abdomen to give energy to the voice − don't just bellow.

Pay attention also to the acoustic properties of the venue. A large echoey church, for instance, will really test the crispness of your consonants. In order to prevent your words from becoming a mush, you'll need to give them extra emphasis, and slow your pace.

If you were addressing a gathering across a playing field, both consonants and vowels would need to be accentuated, and you'd need an extra push from the abdominal and diaphragmatic muscles.

I mentioned imagination a few paragraphs ago. This can be employed in another way for the purpose of achieving confidence. Simply *look* confident. As William James, the father of American psychology, said, 'Act as if'. The chances are that you're faking that confidence at first, but you'll soon feel a return from your audience as they become more at ease with and confident in you. This leads to more confidence on your part. It's what you might call a positive feedback loop.

Once you've made the first speech, confidence will be so much easier to summon the next time.

8.

GO ON – GIVE IT A GO!
A few practice exercises

If you've managed to follow my earlier suggestion, and read aloud whenever it's been convenient to do so, then you'll already have had a good deal of practice. As I said at the beginning, I've tried to write in a style that lends itself to reading aloud: the use of contractions, for instance, and largely avoiding sentences that are cluttered with subordinate clauses.

But some of the passages in this chapter will be harder, because not all of them have been written with the spoken word in mind.

Also, some will be in a language unfamiliar to our everyday ears – oh, it's English all right, but not the English we speak now. You'll find some verse from bygone ages, including some Shakespeare, and there'll be the odd Bible passage – from the Authorised Version!

This will test your powers of presentation to the utmost. Not only will you be making these passages make sense to you, but also to someone else – your listener.

If you can actually have a listener in the room, then so much the better. If not, don't worry too much. Use your taperecorder and listen back *critically*.

You'll notice that your efforts to bring some vocal sense

to the words will enhance your own understanding. It would be far better if you didn't rehearse the passages first silently in your mind, but plunged straight in. This is called sight reading, and forms a part of most if not all speech examinations.

As you become more adept at sight reading, you'll be able to stand in front of an audience, holding your book comfortably in front of you, and read a passage aloud while glancing up at your listeners every few seconds to maintain eye contact.

You must have seen a newsreader on television who's had a late item handed to him and hasn't had the benefit of the teleprompt device or Autocue. He'll look down at the paper, up at the camera, back at the paper and so on.

The trick is to read four or five words ahead of your voice. Soon, you find yourself interpreting each phrase before the words are formed in your mouth. And it gives you those few brief seconds every so often to glance at your listeners.

Even if you don't expect ever to have to do this, the practice here will help your mental agility, and that's always a good thing when it comes to shaping good speech, even in general conversation.

First, imagine you're giving a short speech of welcome for a visiting speaker to a club you belong to. For this one, stand as though you were, indeed, making a speech, and try to take in your imaginary audience with the occasional sweep of your eyes. Take your time. Don't be afraid to pause. A pause to you, the speaker, always sounds longer than it does to an audience.

Ladies and Gentlemen,
Let me begin by quoting from a dictionary. You'll
soon know what it is that's being defined when I tell
you that it's, and I quote, '...sweet, viscid fluid

produced by bees from the nectar collected from flowers.' It is, of course, honey, and something that is very close to the hearts of beekeepers such as ourselves – especially at this time of year when most if not all of us will be preparing to take the crop from the hives. As experienced beekeepers, I suppose we all think we know a fair bit about honey, and we all know that it's far more than what's summed up by that rather cold, clinical definition I quoted a moment ago. But we all know that we can learn more – much more. And we're very fortunate to have with us tonight Mr Harry Mellis, who, as you know, is one of the foremost experts on the subject of honey. He's been a beekeeper himself for more than thirty years, and during that time he's lectured widely on beecraft in general and honey in particular, not only in Britain but on the continent and in the United States, bringing a wide and comprehensive knowledge of his chosen subject to many societies such as our own. Most of us have read his many books on the subject – and many of our younger members have that pleasure to come. I've known Harry Mellis for a number of years, and we've shared many a glass of warming mead during our endless conversations about the wonderful – some would say magical – properties of honey. Ladies and Gentlemen, please welcome Mr Harry Mellis.

Simple words, simple phraseology, friendly delivery, nothing too complicated there. Now something a little more difficult. It's from a William Hazlitt essay on the subject of style. Hazlitt, who died in 1830, was an English critic and essayist, and friend of Coleridge and Wordsworth.

This is more demanding on you for two reasons:

1. It's written for the printed word and not the human voice, so it won't contain the contractions you've been used to in the style of this book.

2. The style belongs in the last century, so won't be as familiar as 1990s speech.

Sit or stand for this one. If you choose to sit, adopt a comfortable but reasonably straight posture that won't restrict any air passages. You'll also need plenty of breath, and to remember what we learned about looking for places for natural pause, because in this piece there are some fairly long sentences.

It is not easy to write a familiar style. Many people mistake a familiar for a vulgar style, and suppose that to write without affectation is to write at random. On the contrary there is nothing that requires more precision, and, if I may so say, purity of expression, than the style I am speaking of. It utterly rejects not only all unmeaning pomp, but all low cant phrases, and loose unconnected slipshod allusions. It is not to take the first word that offers, but the best word in common use; it is not to throw words together in any combinations we please, but to follow and avail ourselves of the true idiom of the language.

To write a genuine familiar or truly English style is to write as anyone would speak in common conversation who had a thorough command and choice of words, or who could discourse with ease, force, and perspicuity, setting aside all pedantic and oratorical flourishes. Or, to give another

illustration, to write naturally is the same thing in regard to common conversation as to read naturally is in regard to common speech.

It does not follow that it is an easy thing to give the true accent and inflection to the words you utter, because you do not attempt to rise above the level of ordinary life and colloquial speaking. You do not assume, indeed, the solemnity of the pulpit, or the tone of stage declamation; neither are you at liberty to gabble on at a venture without emphasis or discretion, or to resort to vulgar dialect or clownish pronunciation. You must steer a middle course. You are tied down to a given and appropriate articulation, which is determined by the habitual associations between sense and sound, and which you can only hit by entering into the author's meaning, as you must find the proper words and style to express yourself by fixing your thoughts on the subject you have to write about.

Anyone may mouth out a passage with a theatrical cadence, get upon stilts to tell his thoughts; but to write or speak with propriety and simplicity is a more difficult task. Thus it is easy to affect a pompous style, to use a word twice as big as the thing you want to express: it is not so easy to pitch upon the very word that exactly fits it. Out of eight or ten words equally common, equally intelligible, with nearly equal pretensions, it is a matter of some nicety and discrimination to pick out the very one the preferableness of which is scarcely perceptible, but decisive.

After you've done it once, you'll find it easier a second time, but the real test is the first. Do, by all means, give it a second go, though, marking places where you think you could have given a little more or less emphasis the last time, or perhaps sped up or slowed down the pace a little, used a harsher consonantal attack to make a point, changed pitch to give a subtle sub-meaning, paused before or after a word.

You can make yourself more aware of these factors by using gestures as you read. I've seen disc jockeys in radio studios who, although talking to a sponge-covered piece of metal with a cable coming out of it, make hand and arm gestures as though someone were sitting in the studio with them. It makes all the difference, and, as we discussed earlier, we must remember that we *are* a voice, we *are* a means of expression, and not merely the possessors of these qualities.

Now some verse. Let's start with an evocative poem by D H Lawrence, called *Piano*. As you read, put yourself in a nostalgic mood by thinking, perhaps, of a scene from your own childhood that conjures up poignant memories. Feel that this emotion is flowing out with the spoken word.

> Softly, in the dusk, a woman is singing to me;
> Taking me back down the vista of years, till I see
> A child sitting under the piano, in the boom of
>   the tingling strings
> And pressing the small, poised feet of a mother
>   who smiles as she sings.
> In spite of myself, the insidious mastery of song
> Betrays me back, till the heart of me weeps to
>   belong
> To the old Sunday evenings at home, with winter
>   outside
> And hymns in the cosy parlour, the tinkling
>   piano our guide.
> So now it is vain for the singer to burst in clamour
> With the great black piano appassionato. The
>   clamour

Of childish days is upon me, my manhood is cast
Down in the flood of remembrance, I weep like a
   child for the past.

There's a great deal of pleasure to be had from reading
good verse aloud, and it's always good practice for the
voice. The next one has humour and dialogue, so you'll
need to think about the inflections you'll use to get that
humour across to a listener. It's called *A Hat Retrieved* by
James and Horatio Smith. Note that this was written in the
first half of the nineteenth century, and the style is not what
you'd expect today.

Pat Jennings in the upper gallery sat,
But, leaning forward, Jennings lost his hat;
Down from the gallery the beaver flew,
And spurned the one to settle in the two.
How shall he act? Pay at the gallery door
Two shillings for what cost, when new, but four?
Or till half-price, to save his shilling, wait,
And gain his hat again at half past eight?
Now, while his fears anticipate a thief,
John Mullens whispered, 'Take my
   handkerchief.'
'Thank you,' cries Pat; 'but one won't make a
   line.'
'Take mine,' cried Wilson; and cried Stokes,
   'Take mine.'
A motley cable soon Pat Jennings ties,
Where Spitalfields with real India vies.
Like Iris' bow down darts the painted clue,
Starred, striped and spotted, yellow, red and
   blue,
Old calico, torn silk, and muslin new.
George Green below, with palpitating hand,

Loops the last kerchief to the beaver's band —
Up soars the prize! The youth, with joy
   unfeigned,
Regained the felt, and felt what he regained;
While to the applauding galleries grateful Pat
Made a low bow, and touched the ransomed hat.

The trick with the next one is to avoid sounding
monotonous with the oft-repeated 'no'. Take your time and
enjoy it. It's called, simply, *No*, by Thomas Hood.

No sun — no moon!
No morn — no noon —
No dawn — no dusk — no proper time of day —
No sky — no earthly view —
No distance looking blue —
No road — no street — no 't'other side the way' —
No end to any Row —
No indications where the Crescents go —
No top to any steeple —
No recognitions of familiar people —
No courtesies for showing 'em —
No knowing 'em!
No travelling at all — no locomotion,
No inkling of the way — no notion —
'No go' — by land or ocean —
No mail — no post —
No news from any foreign coast
No Park — no Ring — no afternoon gentility —
No company — no nobility —
No warmth, no cheerfulness, no healthful ease,
No comfortable feel in any member —
No shade, no shine, no butterflies, no bees,
No fruits, no flowers, no leaves, no birds —
November!

Let's look now at a Thomas Hardy poem. The narrative has an easy flow and doesn't have the strict prosodic form of some verse. You can detect, though, a pattern in the stresses: four in each of the first four lines of each stanza, and three in the last. Try to feel the difference between the images of the second line of the first stanza, in which he speaks of the 'pelting storm', and the very contrasting images of the next line, in which we meet 'the hansom's dry recess'. The poem is called *A Thunderstorm In Town*.

> She wore a new 'terra-cotta' dress,
> And we stayed, because of the pelting storm,
> Within the hansom's dry recess,
> Though the horse had stopped; yea, motionless
> We sat on, snug and warm.
>
> Then the downpour ceased, to my sharp sad pain,
> And the glass that had screened our forms before
> Flew up, and out she sprang to her door:
> I should have kissed her if the rain
> Had lasted a minute more.

It shouldn't be too difficult to find pieces of prose and verse around you for practice.

Before we move onto what you may consider the most difficult of all, let's go to Oscar Wilde's *The Harlot's House*, a particularly poignant piece that wouldn't seem out of place ninety or a hundred years later. Its rhythms take you along, but the point of this exercise is that you mustn't let rhythm take over at the expense of meaning. Enjoy it, and allow it to make your spine tingle a little.

> We caught the tread of dancing feet,
> We loitered down the moonlit street,
> And stopped beneath the harlot's house.
>
> Inside, above the din and fray,
> We heard the loud musicians play
> The *Treues Liebes Herz* of Strauss.

Like strange mechanical grotesques,
Making fantastic arabesques,
The shadows raced across the blind.

We watched the ghostly dancers spin
To sound of horn and violin,
Like black leaves wheeling in the wind.

Like wire-pulled automatons,
Slim silhouetted skeletons
Went sidling through the slow quadrille.

They took each other by the hand,
And danced a stately saraband;
Their laughter echoed thin and shrill.

Sometimes a clockwork puppet pressed
A phantom lover to her breast,
Sometimes they seemed to try to sing.

Sometimes a horrible marionette
Came out, and smoked its cigarette
Upon the steps like a live thing.

Then, turning to my love, I said,
'The dead are dancing with the dead,
The dust is whirling with the dust.'

But she — she heard the violin,
And left my side, and entered in:
Love passed into the house of lust.

Then suddenly the tune went false,
The dancers wearied of the waltz,
The shadows ceased to wheel and whirl.

And down the long and silent street
The dawn, with silver-sandalled feet,
Crept like a frightened girl.

I'll stay with Wilde for one more exercise — an exercise of prose reading. He was, not surprisingly, a bit miffed with Bosie while he languished in prison, and his *De Profundis* makes this clear. Indulge yourself in a little of the poet's invective …

> **… I have no doubt that in this letter in which I have to write of your life and of mine, of the past and of the future, of sweet things changed to bitterness and of bitter things that may be turned into joy, there will be much that will wound your vanity to the quick. If it prove so, read the letter over and over again till it kills your vanity. If you find in it something of which you feel that you are unjustly accused, remember that one should be thankful that there is any fault of which one can be unjustly accused … If you go complaining to your mother, as you did with reference to the scorn of you I displayed in my letter to Robbie, so that she may flatter and soothe you back into self-complacency or conceit, you will be completely lost. If you find one false excuse for yourself, you will soon find a hundred, and be just what you were before. Do you still say, as you said to Robbie in your answer, that I 'attribute unworthy motives' to you? Ah! you had no motives in life. You had appetites merely. A motive is an intellectual aim. That you were 'very young' when our friendship began? Your defect was not that you knew so little about life, but that you knew too much … With very swift and running feet you had passed from Romance to Realism. The**

gutter and the things that live in it had begun to fascinate you ...

And so it goes on. If you can lay your hands on a copy of his complete works, you'll find there this long and bitter letter, which lends itself so well to being read aloud beause of the emotions you'll find there, and the feeling that you're actually speaking to someone else — as, indeed, Wilde was.

Something a little more difficult now. A couple of passages from the Authorised Version of the Bible. As I said earlier, this sort of exercise presents you with the challenge of making sense of the piece not only to yourself as you read it (without previous, silent, rehearsal, I hope) but to someone else who might be listening. Try it as sight-reading at first — that is, without any peeping. Then you can use it as practice for adding some vocal embellishments. The opening lines of St John's gospel have always been a favourite of mine. One word of warning though: it's easy to slip into a pulpit-style oration and parsonical intonations, which should be avoided. You're not, after all, reading this in church, but to your friend or taperecorder. Feel the drama in the words, speaking those that require a soft delivery softly, and giving more oomph to those passages that cry out for a more dynamic declamation.

In the beginning was the Word, and the Word was with God, and the Word was God. The same was in the beginning with God. All things were made by him; and without him was not any thing made that was made. In him was life; and the life was the light of men. And the light shineth in darkness; and the darkness comprehended it not.

There was a man sent from God, whose name was John. The same came for a witness, to bear witness

of the Light, that all men through him might believe. He was not that Light, but was sent to bear witness of that Light. That was the true Light, which lighteth every man that cometh into the world. He was in the world, and the world was made by him, and the world knew him not. He came unto his own, and his own received him not. But as many as received, to them gave he power to become the sons of God, even to them that believe on his name: which were born not of blood, nor of the will of the flesh, nor of the will of man, but of God. And the Word was made flesh, and dwelt among us (and we beheld his glory, the glory as of the only begotten of the Father) full of grace and truth.

We're all familiar with the Twenty Third Psalm — especially in the version that's sung as a hymn. Whether you're a believer or not, enjoy the words, as I hope you did with the last passage.

The Lord is my shepherd; I shall not want. He maketh me to lie down in green pastures. He leadeth me beside the still waters. He restoreth my soul. He leadeth me in the paths of righteousness for his name's sake. Yea, though I walk through the valley of the shadow of death, I will fear no evil: for thou art with me; thy rod and thy staff they comfort me. Thou preparest a table before me in the presence of mine enemies. Thou annointest my head with oil; my cup runneth over. Surely, goodness and mercy shall follow me all the days of my life, and I will dwell in the house of the Lord for ever.

Continuing with language that's unfamiliar, we'll end with two Shakespeare sonnets. The first expresses the writer's regret that the object of his love is so far away and, even though he can get there with the power of his imagination, it irks him that it is but that: imagination. And, because he's made of flesh and blood (or 'earth and water') he's far too substantial to 'leap large lengths of miles'.

> If the dull substance of my flesh were thought,
> Injurious distance should not stop my way;
> For then, despite of space, I would be brought,
> From limits far remote, where thou dost stay.
> No matter then although my foot did stand
> Upon the furthest earth removed from thee;
> For nimble thought can jump both sea and land,
> As soon as think the place where he would be.
> But, ah! thought kills me that I am not thought,
> To leap large lengths of miles when thou art
>   gone,
> But that, so much of earth and water wrought,
> I must attend time's leisure with my moan;
>   Receiving nought by elements so slow
>   But heavy tears, badges of either's woe.

You can afford some vocal extravagance. The poet means you to. You can almost see yourself wagging your finger at 'injurious distance', as though you were saying to it, 'Oh no you *don't* stop my way!' And look at the phrase 'leap large lengths of miles'. Allow your tongue to enjoy those *l*s.

When you come to speak in your work or leisure, perhaps to an audience, remember the power the poet wrings from the words he uses. Not only your choice of words, but the way you deliver them, can be equally powerful, with a little thought. You wouldn't be quite as extravagant in delivery while talking about how to raise money for the organ fund, perhaps, but having that reserve is having at your fingertips − or, more appropriately, your *tongue* tip − the power of persuasion.

The second sonnet is one that most of us are familiar with. Once again, allow yourself the indulgence of being a little extravagant.

> Shall I compare thee to a summer's day?
> Thou are more lovely, and more temperate:
> Rough winds do shake the darling buds of May,
> And summer's lease hath all too short a date.
> Sometime too hot the eye of heaven shines,
> And often is his gold complexion dimm'd;
> And every fair from fair sometime declines,
> By chance or nature's changing course
>   untrimm'd;
> But thy eternal summer shall not fade,
> Nor lose possession of that fair thou owest,
> Nor shall death brag thou wander'st in his
>   shade,
> When in eternal lines to time thou growest;
>   So long as men can breathe, or eyes can see,
>   So long lives this, and this gives life to thee.

And so, as the lover ensures eternal life for his love by the dedication of his lines, which he hopes will be preserved by time, we move on now to our final chapter. The time has arrived for you to put all you've learned into practice, as we look at the big day − the day you may be called upon to make a speech.

9.

UNACCUSTOMED AS I AM
Social speaking

I've deliberately left public speaking until last, because the book is mainly about giving the voice a workout. You should by now have found new possibilities in your voice, and have begun to see it as just as important an expression of what you are as your appearance is.

But many of you will have picked up this book having in mind that almost inevitable occasion when you will have to 'say a few words'. This chapter will help you. But it can be only a brief guide and a number of useful tips, because it is, after all, only a chapter and not an entire book. And there are excellent books on the subject to be had from your bookshop or local library.

One of the first responses you feel when asked to get on your feet is a fluttering in the tummy. We *all* feel that, and it's nothing to worry about. It's quite natural, and gears you up for the task ahead. Anyway, those butterflies will soon be put to rest, because you now know what are the major causes of lack of confidence. We've looked at those in Chapter Seven.

So the day has arrived, and you have your notes in your hand and you walk onto the conference platform, or take your place at the head table at a wedding, or get onto your feet in the works canteen to make the presentation to an old and loved colleague who's retiring or going off to pastures new. You're full of confidence, because you're well prepared. You know you'll be able to speak clearly and that you'll be heard.

But let's go back a few days to see what other preparation you should have made.

WHAT DO YOU WANT YOUR SPEECH TO ACHIEVE?

An obvious question, and one that's so often neglected. Many speeches have been delivered that have left the audience feeling that they've been entertained perhaps, maybe even informed a little, but asking the question, 'What did she actually *say*?'

So have in mind right from the start what you want your speech to achieve. Certainly, you'll need to inform. Yes, you'll need to add a little leaven in the form of some humour. You will, of course, wish to observe the usual courtesies so that you come over as friendly and polite. But you need to have firmly in mind, right through your preparation and delivery, just what result you want your speech to achieve. It may be an appeal for funds for your organisation. It may be that you're a safety officer and you wish to get over to your fellow employees in no uncertain terms that particular practices are fatal and should be avoided. You may be a fire prevention officer talking to schoolchildren on November 3rd or 4th, pleading for good sense and a safety code when they come to light their fireworks on Guy Fawkes Night.

Keep your purpose in mind, and every so often in your preparation ask yourself if you're deviating too much from your original intention. Let purpose lead your speech and determine its progress from beginning to end. Let the purpose show unashamedly at several key points throughout, and let it remain with your listeners after you've finished talking and sat down, by ensuring that it's clearly stated again at the end.

Right, you know *why* you want to say it; now consider *what* to say. You'll need to jot headings down on a piece of paper detailing the main areas you wish to cover. Let's take an example. You're a senior official of a fictitious organisation we'll call the National Badger Foundation, which rescues badgers from the cruel practice of badger-baiting and nurses them back to health in members' homes, as well as campaigning against the barbarism that masquerades under the name of sport.

You're addressing a gathering and, let's make no bones about it, you're after their money. You need funds so that your work might continue.

Your purpose, then, is clear. In achieving your purpose, you'll need to inform. But in what order? Well, let's start by telling them what happens to the wretched creatures when they're dug out of their setts and the dogs are allowed at them. You'll want, perhaps, to quote some statistics in order to intensify in your listeners' minds the feeling of revulsion you're already engendering. So you tell them that X hundred such incidents occur every week in Blankshire alone.

Your next point could be what happens to those who're caught — but you'll then go on to bemoan the fact that far, far too few of the culprits are ever brought to book. And far, far too few of the incidents are ever noticed, leaving injured badgers and orphaned families all over the countryside.

Your next point may be that it costs this much or that much to train one of your organisation's wardens to patrol large areas of countryside and look for the evidence. Again, you'll probably use statistics to show how many badgers *could* be saved with the addition of Y wardens at a cost of Z.

Marshall all these facts, and add them to your notes, and soon you'll see a structure begin to suggest itself.

You'll notice that it wasn't far into the speech structure

that you brought up the question of funds. You would then go on, perhaps, to enlighten your listeners as to how the cash you mentioned was actually spent. Each warden needs a two-week residential course in West Wales and has to attend special one-day seminars quite frequently. Special vehicles are needed, kitted out with detection equipment such as infra-red cameras.

In this example, you are the expert. Chances are that you'll need to do *little* research. But supposing you've been asked to give a speech on something you're *not* expert at — perhaps to propose a toast at a dinner given by the local branch of a cancer research organisation. Here's where you'll need to research your subject well.

Such a speech won't be intended to *inform* these people; after all, they *are* the organisation. But nor would you launch into a discourse on whippet breeding or clay pigeon shooting at such a gathering, or any other irrelevant subject. No one will expect you to be an *expert* on the cancer group, of course, but you'll do well to be able to make references — in the course of your generous praise for the group's work — to some aspects of that work, perhaps trotting out some examples of how it's helped specific people you know of or have read about.

So research your subject by finding some details about its work in the library or by acquiring brochures about it. This shouldn't be too difficult to accomplish. Your local newspaper office may be able to help.

(If you decide you'd like to be a *regular* speaker, you'll soon realise that you'll need to do this type of research often, and you'll build up a good base of contacts. Why not begin now? A card index file is all you need, or a sturdy thumb-index book for alphabetical listing and cross-referencing. You will also need a box of stiff envelopes in which to keep information you've gathered on various subjects that you think you may need to speak about. Your

indexing system will give you an instant location — be it the
library, your own cuttings file, your bookshelves or a person
or organisation — for any given piece of information. It's
surprising how quickly such a system can build up, and it'll
cost you nothing except the price of envelopes.)

Once you've assembled your notes, you'll need to transfer
prompts onto small cards, which you'll have with you on the
rostrum or top table. Never be afraid to let these be seen.
From your hours of patient building, you'll have a pretty
good idea by now of what you're going to say, and the notes
will be merely a prod to ensure you don't go astray. (See
Delivering from Notes on page 112.)

VISUAL AIDS

Visual aids aren't essential, but few talks such as the one
outlined here would survive without them. A
straightforward speech introducing a guest speaker would
rarely need such aids.

What sorts of visual aids are available, and how should
you use them? Flip-charts are a common and popular form.
One page is simply flipped back and over the board that's
holding it, to reveal another beneath.

Then there are the overhead projector and the slide show,
not to mention the video. But a word of warning: visual aids
of *any* type can look distinctly tatty if you don't take care
to remain within your capabilities. If you're not an
accomplished maker of videos, don't go out with the
camcorder and shoot your subject matter, unless you're
absolutely sure the material is (a) absolutely necessary and
(b) will pass muster before an audience. You may find that
stills will do just as well in the form of slides — and you
do have the advantage of being able to keep them on the
screen for as long as you wish while you speak on that
particular aspect of your subject or are answering questions.

Do aim for visual aids, though, whenever it's practicable

to do so. Science has shown that most information is taken in through our eyes, and using pictures of some sort to back up what you're saying will consolidate that information in the minds of your listeners.

PARTS OF SPEECH

No, I don't mean in the grammatical sense: I'm talking about the actual parts of your speech. There's an old saying about how to make a speech.

1. Tell 'em what you're going to tell 'em;
2. Tell it to 'em;
3. Tell 'em what you've just told 'em.

It's not as silly as it sounds. By far the biggest part of your speech is going to be Part Two — the *body* of the speech. Part One, of course, will be an introduction, will outline some of what you're going to say; and Part Three will sum up and end. This final part is known as the peroration. You can't go far wrong if you stick to the formula outlined above.

Think carefully about your opening — and think carefully about your closing. Your opening will arrest your audience if it's been planned well, will whet their appetites for what's to come. The peroration will be the last thing they remember about your speech. It's your big chance to drive your point home. Don't waste it.

TYPES OF SPEECH

Regular speakers are usually those who belong to organisations of one sort or another. In a typical meeting of, say, an enthusiasts' organisation you might find a chairman or -woman introducing a speaker, and then a member of the club proposing a vote of thanks from his seat in the audience.

You've seen an example of the introductory type of

speech in Chapter Eight. We've touched on the speaker's address earlier in this chapter. The proposer of a vote of thanks has little to say, but he's charged with sending the speaker away feeling that he's been appreciated, and winding up that part of the proceedings.

So it's the proposer's job to listen intently to the speaker's words, because he'll need to make a brief reference here and there. The proposer's short speech, therefore, can't be written out beforehand.

This is not to rule out some preparation, however. He may wish to do a little minor research on the subject of, say, the honeybee, and throw in an anecdote. But the essence of his speech is that it be short and to the point, so, if you *do* have an anecdote, ensure that it's brief and entertaining. If in doubt, leave it out.

Refresh your memory now by looking at that speech of introduction on page 88, and then consider the example below of a typical vote of thanks. You will stand in response to an invitation from the chair.

> **Thank you, Mr Chairman. And thank *you*, Mr Mellis, for telling me a lot of things I didn't know. It just goes to show how vast a subject it is that we're dealing with, and even people such as myself, who've been keeping bees and producing honey for nineteen years, have still so much to learn. I'm sure the rest of your audience found your references to healing with honey just as fascinating as I did, and I was particularly intrigued to learn about some of the properties of honey claimed by some Native American tribes. You've given us a most informative and entertaining talk, and I'm sure my fellow members of the Stratton Hill Beekeepers' Association will join me in saying a very rousing Thank You.**

You see, it's really as simple as that. Never be tempted to try to 'top' the speaker's remarks with any of your own, or to challenge what he's had to say. If the speech has been an absolute disaster from a speaker who's unprepared and ill-informed, don't go over the top with praise, but be as complimentary as you honestly can, and leave the speaker feeling that his efforts have been appreciated.

I won't give examples of social speeches, because there are ample excellent books on the subject if you're so minded to buy one. But so much is commonsense, and a little thought and the observance of a few rules of etiquette should set you right for the occasion.

Among the other speeches you may encounter, of course, are the best man's or the bride's father's speech, that of the groom and, in some cases, the bride. Then there are after-dinner speeches in the forms of toasts to the organisation and to the guests, and responses to those toasts. There is the political speech, which doesn't come in any particular place, because such orations are delivered in all sorts of situations, be it the Palace of Westminster or a local protest rally.

TO READ OR NOT TO READ?

Any book on public speaking will tell you that preparation is vital — not just the preparation of your physical self, which we've been addressing in this book so far, but also the preparation of your material. A word first, though, about how that material will appear when you eventually stand up and glance down at it, and the answer to the question: to read or not to read?

It used to be frowned upon to read a speech from a script. Nowadays, so many people who make speeches are so busy that there's no time to do otherwise. Indeed, some people have their speeches written for them. Politicians are a prime example.

But let's assume you're going to prepare your own speech. Should you write it out, rehearse it and then read it word for word? It's a 'yes and no' answer to that one, I'm afraid. If you're a busy councillor and you're opening a new store this morning, talking to overseas visitors at your city hall at lunchtime and addressing a meeting of the Association of County Councils this afternoon, chances are that you'll read your speeches, because you'll probably have two or three to deliver tomorrow and had just as many to deliver yesterday, leaving little time to learn them.

So let's look first at the speech that is read from the page. All of what's gone before will be just as important here, of course. You must pay particular emphasis to expressiveness, because it's so tempting to allow your beautifully-honed speech to *sound* read. And it shouldn't. It should sound spoken.

So prepare as well as time allows. Rehearse your speech. Read it over and over again. Don't try to stick slavishly to every written word, and have in mind from the start that you're going to use the script as a basis from which to speak. If you have this in mind firmly from the start, you'll be more inclined to deviate from the script now and again for the telling of an anecdote or the addition of an unscripted comment or example.

During these days of rehearsal, make a point of deviating from the script now and again in order to get the hang of it. Mark a couple of points where you feel you'll be able to go off at a slight tangent and perhaps regale your audience with an anecdote or example. This is all good practice for the day when you'll be called upon to make an entirely impromptu speech.

As you go through your script, don't be afraid to change words here and there, or to change entire phrases or sentences if you feel they can be spoken better. If you're fortunate enough to be using a word-processor to type your speeches, you can incorporate these alterations when you next power up your machine and you'll eventually be able to print out a clean copy.

Have the finished product legible. There's nothing worse than having to squint at a piece of paper because you can't read the next word. This is unlikely to happen, anyway, because you'll know both from context and having practised what the word should be. But I'm a great believer in belt *and* braces, and would rather leave nothing to chance.

Devise a series of marks that will tell you whether a word is ending on an upward inflection or a downward one. Underline words that are to be emphasised. If you want to throw in a small laugh for effect, mark it in brackets. The same goes for pauses and gestures.

When you stand and deliver, hold the script in one hand and use the other for gesture. Do practise gesture, because with a scripted speech you'll be less likely to find it happening spontaneously. You have to be something of an actor.

You'll have read your speech over several times before the big day, and probably have heard yourself from tape. Bear in mind all we've learned about expressiveness. In my work as a journalist I've seen Lord Mayors handed speeches by their officials when opening a new hospital wing or switching on the Christmas lights — and it's clear that the councillor has paid no attention whatever to how he or she is going to sound. The speech clearly hasn't even been rehearsed, which is an insult not only to the people gathered to hear the speech but the people the councillor represents.

As you read, look up. Catch the eyes of several of your audience. This will necessitate reading a few words ahead. Practise this at home. It will come, and will soon become second nature. The brain needs that vital second or two to process the information on the page and allow you to deliver it as though it were your own spontaneous outpouring. Your audience shouldn't be able to tell whether you're reading entirely from a script or merely glancing at notes.

The best way to practise this is with some text you're not familiar with — something from today's newspaper, for instance, or a book picked up at random, but which you haven't yet read.

DELIVERING FROM NOTES

You could do this by having written and rehearsed a speech as above, and then discarded the script in favour of notes; or, as we discussed above, you won't have actually written out your exact words, but will have built up your speech by trial and error and ended up with a series of prompt headings on pieces of card.

Always number your cards. If you should drop them or mix them up, it'll be all the more easy to sort them back into your preferred order. Don't be afraid to let the cards be seen, and don't stare at them, but use them merely as prompts, and, once you've refreshed your memory for the next chunk of your speech, look up and maintain eye contact with your audience.

LENGTH OF SPEECHES

'Stand up, speak up and *shut* up' is one maxim. Another is, 'If you don't strike oil in the first ten minutes, stop boring!' In many cases, it's good advice. A short speech is far better than a long one. For one thing, your audience may have become bored before you get to the main point of the speech. The purpose, which we discussed above, may be diluted among so much verbiage, when it needs to stand out in sharp relief.

A good rule of thumb is to allow 10 minutes for an after-dinner speech and about 40 minutes or three-quarters of an hour for a lecture. The introduction of a speaker should take no more than about three or four minutes, and the vote of thanks shouldn't last much more than a minute or 90 seconds.

FORMS OF ADDRESS

In formal speeches, forms of address are better adhered to, even if you consider them pompous. To ignore them on those grounds is to invite ridicule because, unless you explain your reasons for ignoring the accepted form, your audience will merely think you're ignorant.

If you should address the Monarch, you would begin your speech with 'Your Majesty, Mr Chairman ...', as you would if you were addressing the Queen Mother. The Duke of Edinburgh: 'May it please Your Royal Highness, Mr Chairman ...' etc. The Prince of Wales would be treated in the same way, as would the Princess of Wales and immediate members of the Royal Family.

If the Prime Minister is in your audience, say 'Mr [or Madam] Prime Minister'. If a knight is guest of honour, you would begin with 'Sir'. A Duke would receive 'My Lord Duke' or 'Your Grace'; a marquess, 'My Lord Marquess'; a baron, earl or viscount, 'My Lord'.

For an archbishop say 'Your Grace'; a bishop, 'My Lord'.

You would address an ambassador as 'Your Excellency'.

A city has a Lord Mayor and a town has a Mayor. They should be addressed as 'My Lord Mayor' or 'Your Worship' respectively — even if the holder of the office is a woman. Sexist it may be, but that's the way it is. A female Lord Mayor is not to be confused with a Lady Mayoress; the latter is the female consort of the Lord Mayor, and should be addressed 'Lady Mayoress'.

TOPICALITY

Even an old speech you delivered five years ago will need dusting off, and part of that procedure is to check it for out-of-date references and opportunities to inject some topicality into it. If your original speech was about dogs and was delivered before certain breeds were put on a legal blacklist, then you would need to make some reference to this.

You wouldn't mention road safety without a reverent but pertinent reference to that multiple pile-up the other day in which seven people died; and you wouldn't deliver a talk on food without making some reference to that well-known television cook Patty le Maison, who won a major award the other day and was splashed all over the housekeeping magazines.

Whether it's an old speech or new, aim to make reference to something that's been in the news, or concerns the areas in which you're delivering your speech. As every pantomime artist knows, you win hearts by mentioning local place names.

HAVE YOU HEARD THE ONE ABOUT ...?

Humour is fine. It acts as a leaven and serves to add balance to your address — especially if it's a longer one such as an after-dinner speech. But don't use the stand-up comic routine unless you *are* a stand-up comic, and your audience expects you to tell a few. Humour should be an integral part of what you're saying, and should reflect your own personality.

If you're generally a rather staid type, usually fairly studious and not given to loud loquacity, it would look out of place indeed if you suddenly burst into a fusillade of quick-fire gags. Your audience may laugh — but not in the way you intended.

Gentle humour is the thing. Weave it into your speech. It'll usually be in the form of anecdote, but not always. Sometimes a simple sentence such as, 'Well, that's what I *thought* she said, anyway' can make a point and raise a laugh. Think carefully about your humour and write the punchline down in full in your notes, plus any other phrases you must speak verbatim. Don't let the joke be lost for want of the definitive wording.

DRINKING

Leave it for the toasts. The best speakers will touch only water before they have to stand up. Afterwards, it's up to you, but you'll still need to be on your best behaviour. It's often thought that a drink will help to calm the nerves. It may — and in some cases a person will be able to have, say, a half of beer or a glass of wine, to calm her nerves and in so doing deliver a good speech.

If you *know* you're one of these people, then take a drink, but with care. If in doubt, don't. Anyway, your nervous energy should be just at the right level for the occasion, and it's likely that you'll be more at your ease by the time you need to get to your feet, because you'll have been chatting to those present.

THE MICROPHONE

Find out beforehand if a microphone is to be provided, and, when you come to use it, don't be like the rock singer and hold it to your lips. It should be set to pick up your voice some distance away from your mouth. In most cases, the public address system will be there to *enhance* your delivery.

I once heard Tony Benn speak. The speaker before him had the mike to his mouth, and the room was awash with popping and feedback. Benn left it on its stand on the table, and it reached to his lower chest. The electronic help, combined with his own good delivery, meant that he could be heard throughout the room perfectly well.

If you get a chance to test the mike beforehand, though, do so.

DRESS SENSE

Your manner of dress should match the occasion. Gone are the days when you had to wear a suit and tie or a formal dress for every speaking engagement. Speakers at rallies have been just as effective in rollneck jumpers and casual trousers as they would have been in suits and ties.

But for most formal and semi-formal occasions you'll need to do as the Romans do, as it were. For dinners, you'll be *told* whether to wear dinner dress or lounge suit, and you'll feel an oaf if you turn up looking the odd one out.

For other occasions, if in doubt, dress as the average person you expect to see at the gathering might *expect* you to dress. That would usually be reasonably smart, with a tie for men and a neat dress or skirt for women. We're back to commonsense again.

DEALING WITH HECKLERS

Have one or two put-downs up your sleeve if you think you may be heckled. But don't use them as soon as a voice is heard from the audience. Use them only if you really have to. Silence is the best repartee in most cases. If that doesn't shut the offending heckler up, then the rehearsed put-down might be used.

Some people will interrupt to make a point. This person isn't, strictly speaking, a heckler and can usually be dealt with by employing a well-chosen remark such as, 'You're quite right to raise that point, and I'll be dealing with it later.'

SINCERITY

Lies will be noticed. Politicians are used to lying in many cases, and are skilled at putting over their points, whether true or false. Most speakers, however, are treated with a little more credulity, and it would be wrong to abuse the trust your audience are putting in you by telling deliberate untruths. Avoid a subject altogether rather than have to lie about it. When you aim to sound sincere, *be* sincere.

DON'T OFFEND

It may seem obvious that you shouldn't offend. But some people may not be aware that they're offending. Know your audience — the *type* of audience you're about to address. It wouldn't do to make light mention of condoms to the Catholic Ladies' Guild or make wisecracks about hamburgers and chips while addressing the Vegan Society.

Ask yourself whether the average member of your audience could be offended by such-and-such a reference. If the answer is yes, leave it out.

SOUND ENTHUSIASTIC

If you truly want your audience to go home feeling that they've had a unique experience, have learned something from you and think you're a jolly good sort, then inject enthusiasm into your delivery. Don't be a David Bellamy or a Magnus Pike. They have their own very enjoyable and informative but nevertheless idiosyncratic way and it wouldn't be wise to try to impersonate them. But they do get 10 out of 10 for enthusiasm when describing their subjects, and you should aim to be just as enthusiastic yourself, even if you don't adopt over-the-top mannerisms or peculiarities of speech.

Such advice, though, must carry the proviso that, if you are naturally like one of the Doctors Bellamy or Pike, then that is your way and you would be ill advised to change. Most of us, however, aren't, and you'll soon discover, as you accept speaking engagements, that you're developing a style that's peculiarly your own.

BODY LANGUAGE

Body language is in operation all the time. We don't

just turn it on when we think it may be useful. Your body will tell the audience that you're dull if you gaze at one space, talk with a monotone and have a glazed look in your eyes. But that's not the sort of body language we should be aiming for.

The body speaks with more than just the voice. The hands and arms are an obvious adjunct to this, as Magnus Pike would no doubt testify. But study the different types of gesture — the expansive sweep of the arm, the frenzied chopping action of the hand, stabbing the air with your finger, the wide shrug, hitting your palm with your fist, holding the hand out palm forward to hush the audience and prepare them for something special. The combinations are endless.

Watch seasoned speakers on television or at dinners. Watch not only their hands and arms, but their eyes, the movements of their heads. Don't forget to smile — but don't deliver the whole speech with a silly grin. Allow your face to express the emotions it would if you were talking to just one person. If it remains stationary, your enthusiasm for your subject will be put seriously in doubt.

IN GOOD VOICE

And that brings us back to the voice. If it's used effectively in conjunction with all the tips and techniques discussed in this chapter, you have a formidable armoury, which you can test now by going back to the piece of text I asked you to record at the beginning of the book, and comparing the second version with the first.

It goes without saying that you'll by now have improved your delivery and made yourself more aware of the vocal techniques at your disposal to bring out emotions of every hue, to charm, to raise to anger, to cajole, to comfort, to inform, to educate, to entertain.

Be clear and crisp, remember the expressiveness that can

be achieved with rising and falling inflection, the intelligent use of pausing and pointing, rises and falls in volume and pitch.

Care for your voice as you do your face and hair, your dress. Exercise it frequently by using texts, some favourite, some untried. It's a glorious part of your being, just as your body is. And, like your body, it needs a workout now and then.

GLOSSARY

ABDOMINAL   Of the abdomen or belly, signifies healthy, deep breathing that expands the belly area rather than just the chest.

ALVEOLAR RIDGE   The hard ridge just behind the top front teeth.

BLADE   Part of tongue just behind the tip.

CLAVICULAR   Of the clavicle, or collarbone, applied to shallow breathing that tends to raise the upper chest instead of filling the whole trunk.

CONSONANTS   Sounds that aren't vowels or vowel sounds, e.g. **p, b, d, f**; made by the coming together of two organs of articulation such as the lips or the tongue and teeth, trapping or partially trapping air that seeks to be expelled.

CONTINUANTS   Consonants that aren't plosives, allowed to continue without impediment, such as **n, l, r.**

DIPHTHONG   Sound made of two vowel sounds, such as the **a** and **oo** that make the **ow** in 'cow'.

FRAENUM   The small fold of skin beneath the tongue.

FRICATIVE   Of a consonant whose utterance partly traps air and lets it out with friction, such as **f**.

GLOTTAL STOP   Sometimes called glottal shock or glottal attack, the partial holding back of air in the glottis often at the beginnings of vowels.

GLOTTIS   The space between the vocal cords — see **Larynx**.

INTERCOSTALS   Or 'intercostal muscles' — the muscles between the ribs.

LABIAL   Of the lips — **m** is a bi-labial consonant.

LARYNX   Often called the voicebox or Adam's apple, the part of the throat that contains the vocal cords.

NASAL   Of the nose; a consonant made by the flow of air down the nose, such as **n** and **m**.

NASALITY   Either over- or under-use of the nasal passages in speech, producing a 'twang' or a 'cold-in-the-nose' effect respectively.

PALATE

Soft is towards the back, hard is towards the front. See **Velum**.

PLOSIVES

Consonants that issue a small explosion when uttered, such as **p, b, t, d, k** and **g.**

PROJECTION

Art of making one's voice heard at a distance by the use of good breathing and muscle control rather than shouting.

RESONATORS

Spaces that amplify sound through resonance, such as the chest, pharynx, mouth cavity and sinuses; also the box of a guitar or other string instrument.

SIBILANCE

Characterised by an over-produced s; a hissing.

SINUSES

Cavities, recesses or passages in the skull; see **Resonators.**

TRACHEA

Wind pipe.

TRIPHTHONG

Sound made of three vowel sounds, such as the **a, oo** and neutral vowel in 'hour'.

UNVOICED

See **Voiced**.

UVULA	Dangling fold of flesh at the back of the mouth.
UVULAR	Of the uvula or the area surrounding it.
VELUM	Soft palate.
VOICED	Uttered using vocal intonation − **d**, for instance, as opposed to its *un*voiced equivalent, **t**.
VOWELS	Sounds that are not consonants, e.g. **a, e, i, o, u,** but also taken to mean vowel sounds. See **Diphthong** and **Triphthong**.

INDEX

RIGHT WAY
PUBLISHING POLICY

HOW WE SELECT TITLES

RIGHT WAY consider carefully every deserving manuscript. Where an author is an authority on his subject but an inexperienced writer, we provide first-class editorial help. The standards we set make sure that every **RIGHT WAY** book is practical, easy to understand, concise, informative and delightful to read. Our specialist artists are skilled at creating simple illustrations which augment the text wherever necessary.

CONSISTENT QUALITY

At every reprint our books are updated where appropriate, giving our authors the opportunity to include new information.

FAST DELIVERY

We sell **RIGHT WAY** books to the best bookshops throughout the world. It may be that your bookseller has run out of stock of a particular title. If so, he can order more from us at any time—we have a fine reputation for "same day" despatch, and we supply any order, however small (even a single copy), to any bookseller who has an account with us. We prefer you to buy from your bookseller, as this reminds him of the strong underlying public demand for **RIGHT WAY** books. Readers who live in remote places, or who are housebound, or whose local bookseller is unco-operative, can order direct from us by post.

FREE

If you would like an up-to-date list of all **RIGHT WAY** titles currently available, please send a stamped self-addressed envelope to

ELLIOT RIGHT WAY BOOKS, KINGSWOOD, SURREY, KT20 6TD, U.K.